Things I don't get,

WHICH ARE A LOT!

(Humorous observations of things around me as I get older)

Lawrence W. Perkins

To my Wife, Kathie - I'm so glad I found You!
Thanks for Loving me!

To my Daughter Kim and my Son Andy –
I'm so very proud of you and I love you very much!

Foreword (and Forewarned)

I never pictured myself as someone who would face 'getting older' gracefully. Heck, I never even saw myself getting old at all! The whole process happened in the blink of an eye. It kind of reminds me of a line from "My Generation" by the Who – "I hope I die before I get old". Now I really know what they meant about thinking and acting like an older person. If you don't know who Roger Daltrey and Pete Townsend are, you're way too young to be interested in this book. David Crosby, Stephen Stills, Graham Nash, and Neil Young suggested in "Suite: Judy Blue Eyes"- "Do not let the past remind us of what we are not now". Later on, in "Teach your Children", they sang, "And so, become yourself, because the past is just a goodbye". This is but a glimpse into some of the music I enjoyed listening to while in college.

I always saw the humor in most everything life had to offer and that sure hasn't changed as I've aged. It feels like there will always be an 18-year-old kid inside me who wonders what he wants to be when he grows up and will not hesitate to try things he used to be able to do. Partly because, as we age, we want to believe we can still be useful (pride) and partly because we don't want to pay someone else good money to do something we really are still capable of doing ourselves (cheap). This comes, in part, from watching my 80-year-old father climb up on the roof to clean out the gutters. In my sleep I hear my Mother (or is it my wife?) yelling "what do you think you're doing – you're going to kill yourself".   Or "why don't you call someone who actually knows what they're doing", or the final straw, "don't expect me to drive you to the hospital!"

Television brought lots of very funny and talented comedians into our homes. I was greatly influenced by Groucho Marx, Henny Youngman, Rodney Dangerfield, Joan Rivers, Mel Brooks, George Burns, Jerry Stiller, Don Rickles, Jonathan Winters, Jerry Seinfeld, Steve Martin, George Carlin, and, Robin Williams, among many, many others.   Andy Rooney had an especially interesting and fresh perspective on life as well. I enjoyed his take on things. His 'what if' approach made me think 'outside the box'.

Before they made their early movies for Paramount Pictures, the Marx Brothers would take their Broadway plays on the road around the country to see which gags got the best laughs. The funniest bits stayed in and others were discarded. In a similar fashion, I've tried out some of this material on friends and if they thought it funny, it made the final cut.

I grew up in a very culturally diverse middle-class neighborhood.   In an odd way, this contributed to my sense of humor. We had our own mini melting pot – a microcosm of our larger America in the 1950's. Many of my childhood friends were Jewish, Polish, Armenian, Italian, Asian, you name it, we had it. It really made life interesting and formative for me as a kid. I found just listening to them talk about everyday life made me laugh – they were funny without trying to be (probably why I later enjoyed the Seinfeld sit-com so much). Their thought process, perspective, and life experiences, gave me a different slant on things. They were also very warm, inviting and caring individuals. I came to admire and respect them very much, for many reasons.

Most of our Moms stayed home, managed the household, and kept an eye on their kids. We played after school at each other's homes, so we really got to interact with the different ethnic groups in their own environments. Many of our grandparents were first generation immigrants who lived with their son's or daughter's families, so we got to know them as well. Each visit was unique - like a sketch or episode in a never ending, real life sit-com. I now wish I had the forethought to write them down. Some of the older relatives yelled all the time, even if they weren't mad (or hard of hearing). The whole thing was hilarious to me, although I never let on, and the 'old school' culture was charming and precious! "Irving, that roasted duck has been sitting out on the kitchen counter for hours now. If I eat it, I'll get botulism and die, so put it in the ice box already!" Nobody thought this stuff was humorous but me. Or, "it's not like in the old days…" Or, "Aunt Mabel would be turning over in her grave if she could see what's going on today". Which leads me to the reason why I decided I just had to write this silly book. It occurs to me that, like our parents and grandparents maintained, the world has changed – it's not as safe, nurturing, constant, or predictable as before. Maybe it's just a generational deal. Things are different today, however, and, as a result, sometimes I don't get it. **"I tell ya I just don't get it"!** And thus, begins a humorous look (you be the judge) at the changing world around me. I hope you enjoy reading this little book as much as I enjoyed writing it.

Warning: Some of the observations that follow require a strong 'tongue-in-cheek' approach and perspective, not to be confused with 'foot-in-mouth' disorder. At best, my writing style resembles a "stream of unconsciousness", if you will (my apologies to James Joyce).

When I was a kid …

Growing up in America during the 1950's, our nurturing parents repeatedly gave us lots of advice. I think of them as 'Words of Wisdom'. Here are some favorites:

"Clean your plate, there are children starving in China!" I never understood the connection between the two. If I didn't finish everything I was expected to eat, was the remaining food immediately air lifted to those poor Chinese kids on the other side of the world? Who came to pick up my uneaten food? What about other kids elsewhere? It made me feel I was somehow responsible for their regrettable present situation. Because of the associated guilt I harbored, my compliance only resulted in becoming overweight.

"Make sure you're wearing clean underwear; you might get in an accident!" It's clear they were always thinking ahead. Did my parents honestly think doctors or nurses even cared about the condition of my underwear? Was the hospital staff required to fill out a form describing the status of my under-garments? Would they refuse treatment if we had 'soiled' underwear? Would this vital information get back to our neighbors or relatives? Today, it would probably be immediately posted on Facebook!

"Just look at that dirt on the back of your neck (or behind your ears)!" Did they really expect us kids to conveniently carry a mirror with us - because without one, it's physically impossible to view the 'back of your neck'? Did they think we could turn our heads around like an owl? Did this statement infer the rest of our bodies were, in fact, clean by comparison? Were we supposed to remember and explain how the dirt got there? I think they were afraid someone would see our disgusting condition and it would be a reflection on my mother being a bad parent. Lots of guilt going around. Again, today it would result in a bath followed by comments on social media.

"If you don't stop crossing your eyes, they will get stuck like that!" I once asked an optometrist to verify if that were true. He hesitated, then said, "Probably not". He was a smart guy. His answer left some room for doubt, didn't completely contradict my folks, and, mostly through fear, assured compliance on my part with their request. Actually, my parents concern was understandable, as I had started wearing glasses at the age of two. I don't think vision insurance was available until years later, so they had to pay for my glasses out of their own pocket. My dad looked at this way: Every time my prescription changed, he had to buy me new glasses – sort of like paying for new shoes as your feet grew. The straw that almost broke the proverbial 'camel's back' was when I needed braces to straighten my teeth and correct an overbite. Between being overweight (due to the children starving in China), the glasses (due to standing on my head to watch television), and the braces (grandma said it was due to sucking my thumb as a baby), I thought DNA testing would surely confirm I had been adopted.   Finally, when I reached the age of 25 or so, my folks put all speculation to rest by assuring me that I was, in fact, their child. I think by then, the damage to my self-esteem had already been done.

"You'll eat it and you'll like it!" This was synonymous with **"don't argue with me!"** and often followed by, **"because I said so, that's why!"**   How could they possibly know that I would 'enjoy' this food? I personally believe it came full circle with the deal about the poor kids starving in China. They felt they were in charge (which, of course, they were) and didn't want to chance their authority being usurped. It also clearly meant it was the end of the discussion (a far cry from the roles played by young children and their parents today!).   I remember especially disliking lima beans.   Once, I actually lined them up in a circumference under and around the edge of my plate to avoid having to eat them. When I started to leave the dinner table, my mother (without turning around) quietly said, "You're not leaving that table, young man, until every one of those are gone." How did she know? From that point on, I figured all women wore long hair to cover up the 'eyes in the back of their head'.   We had a dog named Lance (short for 'Sir Lancelot the Wonder Dog'). Mom proudly told people he had a pedigree and the papers to prove it.   The only papers I ever saw were strewn all over the floor in a failed attempt to potty-train him.   My brothers and I made him psychotic by dressing him up in our sister's underwear and then letting him run wild throughout our neighborhood (it probably had a detrimental effect on my sister as well). Anyway, here's my point. Lance had a very discriminating palate (a picky eater) and time and again disproved the phrase "You'll eat it and you'll like it". My brothers and I conducted taste tasting with ole' Lance. In rapid succession, we tossed him hamburger, hamburger, hamburger, ONION. Every time, he would gulp-down the hamburger and then spit out the onion. Apparently, he didn't 'enjoy' the onion.

There were many wonderful weekly family-oriented TV shows in the 50's when I was growing up. Television was a new phenomenon and method of entertainment. Several come to mind, including; 'Donna Reed', 'Ozzie and Harriet', 'The Real McCoy's', 'My Three Sons', 'Father Knows Best', 'The Honeymooners', 'I Love Lucy', 'Make Room for Daddy', 'Lassie', and, 'Leave it to Beaver'. Their initial and enduring success can be attributed in large part to the creative writers behind the scenes and the many characters they created. In addition, the actors were convincing – many set good examples and almost became role models for us. The story lines were wholesome, reassuring, and taught us lessons about having good morals and respect for others. The script writers espoused timeless values and the characters became synonymous with ideal suburban American family life in the Midwest in our mid-20th century.

Having said that, some aspects weren't very realistic. Even as kids, I think we wondered why Ozzie Nelson was always hanging around the house. Apparently, he didn't have a real job and certainly never went to 'work'. Why was Ward Cleaver the only father in his neighborhood to be counted on to always do the right thing – smoothing things over with the other parents? Why didn't the girls swoon over Ricky Nelson at the malt shop like they did when he sang a new song at the end of the program? Eddie Haskell was clearly a bully to the other little friends of Beaver – think that would be acceptable today? Why were Lucy and Desi's twin beds pushed apart even after 'little Ricki' was born? But you know what, it was OK - a gentler, more sheltering, and somewhat nurturing time in our lives, wasn't it? Execs at the TV stations seemed to care about the same values our parents were trying to instill in us. Probably had something to do with ratings and censorship as well.

In the 1950's, many of us kids were glued to a black and white TV series called "The Adventures of Superman". It was adapted from the original 'Superman' comics and it was great - I couldn't get enough of it. The opening music was thrilling and the lines were equally stirring – down right patriotic in nature: "Faster than a speeding bullet, more powerful than a locomotive, able to leap tall buildings in a single bound... and who, disguised as Clark Kent, mild mannered reporter for a great metropolitan newspaper, fights a never-ending battle for truth, justice, and the

American Way". Why, any kid worth his or her salt could repeat these lines verbatim – undoubtedly still can! "Look, up in the sky, it's a bird, it's a plane, it's Superman!" We certainly didn't dare question any of it at the time, however, 70 years later (through somewhat jaundiced eyes) I find it hard to believe we bought into it, 'hook, line and sinker'. If it was truly a 'never ending battle', didn't he get awfully discouraged? Same deal all the time - saving people and jailing crooks day after day. Why would he stand there while bullets bounced off his chest and then duck when the bad guy threw the empty gun at him? Then there's the bit about the crowd staring up into the sky and wondering what the heck was flying around up there above their heads! If they couldn't differentiate between a plane, a bird, or a human being wearing a cape, they should make an appointment with an optometrist. Last, but certainly not least (and, in my opinion, here's the big one), do glasses really make the man? How could people not recognize that Clark Kent and Superman were one and the same person?? Especially in the case of Perry White, Lois Lane, and Jimmy Olson who worked in the same office with him every day. For heaven's sake, Lois was in love with him and apparently remained forever clueless. Maybe that's why they say, "Love is blind"!

If you were fortunate, you could also take in the black and white 'B' pictures (now called films or movies) running at the local movie theatre on Saturday afternoon. They were called

Saturday matinees. Usually you would get to see 2 movies for 25 cents – sometimes with a cartoon in between. They were very popular, mainly for kids. I'm sure Mom and Dad were pleased that we were out of their hair for a couple of hours. You had to get there early because the line was very long, often running a block or more down the sidewalk outside the show. A man (more than likely the manager) walked up and down the line of kids saying, "Have your money ready and tell the cashier how many". There was a little 'mom and pop' candy store right next door – how convenient.   Most of the pictures shown were westerns or classic horror films like Dracula, Frankenstein, or The Wolf Man.   William Castle (Columbia Films) and Terence Fisher (Hammer Films), among other directors, began cranking out lots of remakes, based on the old standards, in addition to new monster genre films and psychological thrillers which have become cult classics.   My personal favorites included 'The attack of the 50 Foot Woman', 'The Wasp Woman', 'It Came from Beneath the Sea', 'The Creature from the Black Lagoon', 'Tarantula', 'Them', 'The Blob', 'House of Wax,', 'The Tingler', 'The House on Haunted Hill', 'The Fly', and, 'The Colossus that Ate New York' (not sure that was the real title). Flying saucers and aliens from outer space were especially excellent and popular themes. They conjured up images of things that scared you to death and gave you nightmares for weeks. My younger brother even subscribed to the magazine 'Famous Monsters of Film Land'. What I don't get is how did the theatre make any money at 25 cents a head? You'd have to attract 1,000 kids each week just to pay the projectionist, the ushers, the ticket lady, the clean-up crew, and the film distributor - just to break even! Maybe that's why they kept raising the price, first to 35 cents, then 50 cents, and finally $1.00. It got to the point where you had to be a rich kid to go to the Saturday afternoon matinee!

I always had trouble understanding or making any sense of many classic children's stories and nursery rhymes. For example, in 'The Three Little Pigs', why doesn't the Big Bad Wolf simply climb in through the open window rather than all that huffing and puffing? He goes through those stupid antics not once, but three times! In 'The Tortoise and the Hare', how could the rabbit decide to take a nap and fall asleep during their contest? Wasn't it the race of a lifetime – where's his motivation? Did he have insomnia the previous night or did he 'take a dive'? Didn't the people who were betting on the outcome protest, sue, or at least demand a do over? In 'Hansel and Gretel', our worst childhood fears are realized – they are taken into the woods, abandoned by their parents, and left to die. Aren't these guardians the very ones who are supposed to ensure our safety and protect us? Why a trail of bread crumbs? Didn't they realize it would be quickly eaten by the animals in the forest? Apparently, no search party was ever organized, yet they managed to outwit and dispose of the witch and return home again, all by themselves. Weren't the proper authorities ever notified? Why didn't someone distribute 'missing' posters? Did Wolf Blitzer run their story all day long on CNN? Didn't their little chums at school wonder what happened to them? Where were the truant officers? I guess the bus driver never reported them missing either. What I truly don't get is why they went home – weren't they afraid to confront their parents? Surely there was some lack of trust here! In 'Little Red Riding Hood', how could she not recognize the wolf dressed up like her grandmother? Come on now. Was she near sighted or was her grandmother really that ugly? In 'Snow White', the evil queen is able to find her way into the deep woods to locate the seven dwarfs' cottage not once, but three times. All without the benefit of a map or GPS! In 'Rumpelstiltskin', why did the stupid miller brag to the King that his daughter could spin straw into gold in the first place? What a great way to impress the sovereign, right? How did he think he was going to make good on that deal? Kind of put his daughter in a tough place, didn't he? Really, her first born child? Wouldn't her husband have something to say about that arrangement?   By the way, what about the dwarf's side of the bargain in all of this?   Shouldn't he have considered everything involved in raising a kid as a single parent? Why could Jack Sprat not eat fat, nor his wife any lean? Either way, they don't sound like healthy, balanced diets to me – didn't their mothers teach them to eat fruits and vegetables? Were they trying out the first gluten free diets? Sounds like serious eating disorders to me.   At least they seemed good at sharing.

9

Furthermore, if my wife ever caught me 'licking my platter clean', I'd be thrown out of our house for good. What would Emily Post have said about that? What was 'Humpty Dumpty' doing on top of that wall anyway, and how on earth did he get up there? He must have been a real dare-devil or hopefully had great insurance. Actually, the poem doesn't even tell you he was an egg! Why were the Kings men consulted (let alone their horses) about putting him back together again? Didn't the town have a doctor? Why not take him to the nearest hospital or clinic? Now, if they had super glue, he might have survived. Then there's 'Jack and Jill'. I get the fact that part of their chores involved routinely fetching a pail of water. What I don't get is how he managed to jump up and run home after 'breaking his crown'. Fast recovery, eh? Was he taken to the nearest hospital for precautionary x-rays or an MRI to check for concussion? Apparently not, because some woman named old Dame Dob 'patched up his head with vinegar and brown paper' and he was fine. Really? Talk about a weird home remedy! Did anyone tell his parents what had happened? How have these comforting, yet, grotesque, tales persisted for centuries?

I love watching murder mysteries on TV, especially those that take place in England (Midsomer Murders and Father Brown come to mind). Many of these shows are set in tiny, tranquil, bucolic villages. In each episode, someone who lives in the village is murdered and the local constabulary is charged with solving the crime.   What I don't get is if there are twenty episodes in a season and they produce, say, seven seasons, that's a lot of dead people piling up!   At some point the little towns would have more dead citizens than living. Maybe the last episode should involve the last criminal killing the last policeman and then committing suicide. Wouldn't you think the town would have achieved a certain reputation before that actually happened?   Who would dare visit or vacation there, let alone actually live there?   Wouldn't the population be leaving the cursed village in droves?   In the end, there would be no one left to run the town and it would become extinct – a ghost town!

When we were kids, either Gene Autry, Roy Rodgers, or some other famous cowboy used to sing 'Home on the Range' while strumming his guitar as part of his weekly TV program. They sure seemed to lead less stressful lives back then, didn't they? Here's what I don't get about that song. Who played with the deer and antelope? What happened when a grizzly bear or mountain lion strolled by?   Was there instant bloodshed and death?   How far were you from an 'Urgent Care' facility if you were trampled by a buffalo (is it buffalo or bison on the range) stampede?   How close was the nearest fire station if there was a sudden prairie fire?   Why were discouraging words seldom heard, after all, they lived a pretty rugged life filled with serious hardships. If the skies weren't cloudy all day how did they grow their crops without rain? The lyricist sure makes it sound like an idyllic life in a perfect environment, doesn't he? In reality, it couldn't have been all peaches and cream - the average life expectancy was only around 40! My mind always worries about what could happen, which was certainly a lot! By the way, is it just my imagination or is there a bright golden haze on the meadow?

Looking back on my childhood, I'm surprised my siblings and I believed in the reality of Santa Claus, the Tooth Fairy, the Easter Bunny and other make-believe personages for as long as we did. Learning the startling truth was very traumatic for some kids when it eventually happened. May have even scarred them for life! I'm sure the deep-seated memory of this shocking realization has kept the psychiatric trade rolling in dough for years. I can remember my folks making me promise not to tell my brothers or sister once I learned the truth. I never spilled the beans, but, instead, let them find out for themselves in due course. It was a rite of passage among many others in the process of growing up. My wife and I, as did most parents, followed the pattern with our own kid's years later. It was a way, I think, of sheltering, protecting, and preserving the innocence of our children for as long as we could because we knew the world could often be a tough place. Sometimes the truth really does hurt, doesn't it?

When I was around ten or twelve years old, my uncle had a poster of a laughing donkey hanging on a wall in his finished basement. Beneath the donkey was printed, "Why are there so many more horse's asses than there are horses?" All the adults thought it was humorous. My younger brother once asked me what it meant. I couldn't explain it to him then. For different reasons, I still can't explain it now.

I never really understood why we had to have air raid drills in school during the 1950's. I realize that the London Blitz from WWII was still fresh in everyone's mind and the cold war with Russia prompted serious fears of nuclear war – but what good did hiding under your desk or sitting up against a cold, damp wall in the basement with your head tucked between your knees really do anyway? If your school building actually took a direct hit from an A-Bomb you wouldn't stand a chance of surviving – there would only be ashes left afterward. Some people actually built underground bunkers and stocked up on food and water in case of an attack. Most people thought that was pretty extreme. How would you know when it was safe to come out (radiation) and who would be left alive? Whatever happened to all those bunkers anyway? Rod Serling was brilliant at envisioning and developing several weird situations and plots using the nuclear war theme on his TV series, 'The Twilight Zone'. Fire drills I get, air raid drills I don't.

The small brick bungalow I grew up in as a kid had a 'milk chute' by the back door. It was used by our neighborhood 'milkman' to deliver fresh milk and take back the empty bottles. This 'milk chute' had both an inner and outer door which was used to keep the milk and other dairy products cool in the summer and prevented them from freezing during the winter months. In theory, you never really had to come face to face with the actual milkman – in fact some probably didn't even know his name or what he looked like. You just left the money for him in the chute when he came for the empties. We used to tell my younger brother and sister that the milk, butter, eggs, etc. just appeared magically each day if you wished hard enough. I think they finally saw the Twin Pines guy one day and wised up. The more I think about it, any robber with a long arm could have broken into the house and taken everything. My dad was a trusting kind of guy. Times were different back then. Unlike today, you could name every neighbor in every house on the street. You talked to them regularly and knew what was happening in their lives. You weren't afraid to leave your doors unlocked day or night. There was a certain reciprocal bond or feeling of trust between you and the people who lived on your block. Most of the moms didn't work outside their home and were available to help each other – which is probably how we learned what was going on. It was a big deal when someone died or moved away. They say that everything comes full circle in life or there's nothing new under the sun. It makes me chuckle to hear that grocery stores today have recently come up with a novel idea for improving customer convenience – 'home delivery'! The small mom and pop stores were offering that routinely almost a hundred years ago!

In high school, I really enjoyed math classes, especially trigonometry, calculus, and solving algebraic equations. Notwithstanding my enjoyment, one thing used to bug me. Why were we always trying to solve for X, Y, and Z? Hadn't it been done a gazillion times by a gazillion students before me? Wouldn't it have been better if we taught them to solve for themselves? Why did we constantly have to help them out - over and over again? For Heaven's sake, my granddaughter is still working on this same problem in her math class today! Why didn't we turn our attention to the other poor letters long ago? I always felt sorry for them. Why didn't we help A, B, and C? Why were Q, R, and S left out? Was the entire rest of our alphabet to be pitied as unsolvable?   Certainly, it would have given my teachers a welcome break as well.   Maybe X, Y, and Z could step up and teach the others how to solve for themselves!

Remember when many older folks put plastic covers over the seats of their new furniture and doilies on the arms of chairs? If you weren't careful, you could actually slide right off the sofa onto the floor. I get the fact that they were trying to protect or preserve the upholstery. What I don't get is why they never took them off - ever.   After these people died years later, the plastic was still there!   The rest of the fabric was tattered, soiled, and smelly but the seats and arms looked brand new!

Thinking back to when I was a kid, the game of baseball meant everything to me. In part, that was probably because our winter months in Michigan seemed to last forever – we were chomping at the bit once spring and then summer finally arrived. We would play neighborhood 'pick-up' games all day, every day (weather permitting) on our local school ball field, and then have real league games (with actual uniforms) after dinner and on Saturdays. Every guy has his favorite 'baseball movie'. Among the great ones are: The Natural, The Sandlot, A League of Their Own, Eight Men Out, Pride of the Yankees, It Happens Every Spring, 61*, 42, For Love of the Game, and on and on…   Mine is 'Field of Dreams'. Ray Liotta plays Shoeless Joe Jackson in the film and has some lines that resonate strongly with me. "I loved this game – the green grass, the blue sky. I would have played for food money. The roar of the crowd as they rose when the ball was hit deep – Shoot, I'd have played for nothing". I can easily add my own thoughts to his. I still vividly recall the smells of the dirt, linseed oil in your mitt, and the grass stains on my pants. The haze and heat of the mid-day sun and the additional scents of rosin and talc. The sweat on the brim of your cap. The sound and feel of a wooden bat making contact with a leather, red stitched ball – the tingle in your hands when you hit the sweet spot on the bat. The arc of the ball drifting into the outfield - almost in slow motion. Facing a pitcher who had a really good curve ball – and getting a hit off of him. The momentary sting of getting hit by a wild pitch – then rubbing your arm while running down to first base. The cheers and support from your team-mates as you slid into third base – safely. The feel of your spikes as they slammed into and gripped the bag. Sensory moments, forever fixed in your mind – memories of my youth gone by. I often wish I could borrow Mr. Peabody's 'Way Back Machine' and relive just one day on the baseball diamond as a twelve-year-old kid. The game endures, and reminds me of a simpler time – a good time, when our future hopes and dreams lay far ahead of us. It was the BEST, it was perfect! Shoeless Joe asked, "Is this Heaven?" Oh yes, Joe. It's where dreams come true.

Pardon me, what did you say? ...

Whats up with everyone suddenly using the expression 'gone missing' or 'went missing' when the existing, and perfectly adequate word 'disappeared' has been used for years? Likewise, 'went down' or 'gone down' to describe something that simply 'happened' seems unnecessary and verbose as well. Why use two words when one will suffice anyway? The word 'recuse' is suddenly popular in American politics today rather than 'excuse'. By definition, 'recuse' means excusing oneself from involvement or not being qualified to perform legal duties due to possible conflict of interest. Why not just say 'excuse' – it's in the definition anyway! Maybe it's a stronger word or just a fancier word used by lawyers and politicians to sound important or more intelligent than us mere mortals. Then there was the TV program about a patient who was critically 'unwell'. Why not just say he was ill or sick? I'm convinced they're trying to confuse or act superior to us. Another new word being used in social media is 'disinvited'. Shouldn't we still be saying 'uninvited'? How about 'disrespected' – as in, "He disrespected me"? Shouldn't it be, "He didn't respect me" or "He showed me no respect"? Then there's the word 'redacted'. It refers to removing sensitive information from documents. Wouldn't it be simpler to just say 'edited' – who the heck knows what redacted means. I'm not really sure 'gone missing', 'went down', 'disinvite', 'disrespect', or 'redacted' would be considered proper English anyhow – or is that 'anyway'?   Whilst we're on the topic of "The King's English", over the years, a lot has been lost in translation between British terms and their American equivalents – to wit:

British Terminology	American Equivalent
Bob's your Uncle	And there you have it…
Fancy	Like, want, or Desire
Local	Your Favorite Neighborhood Pub
Pub	Public House or Local Tavern
Dog's Bollocks	The Best-Really Fantastic
Knackered	Tired
Bee's Knees	Fabulous
Gob smacked	Amazed
Mate	Friend
Bloke	Man
Football	Soccer
Solicitor/Barrister	Attorney/Lawyer
Nosh	Food
Chips	French Fries
Crisps	Chips
Bitter	Beer

| Bangers and Mash | Sausage and Mashed Potatoes |
| Jacket Potato | Baked Potato |

It would seem the English and Americans have much in common except their language – an observation made by Sir Winston Churchill, I believe. I can remember my dear English Grandfather asking me to hand him a 'spanner' to work under the 'bonnet' of his car. Of course, he meant a 'wrench' to work under the 'hood'– silly me!

Do you think, as I do, that we have drastically overused the phrase 'Breaking News' on TV stations? It was originally meant to draw our attention to something really important or we should be made aware of right away. Now, it covers and includes everything from; some kid fell off his bike, a man locked himself out of his car, it might rain this afternoon, or, Melania Trump is getting her nails done today. Give me a break! Sadly, 'Breaking News' doesn't have the impact it used to for me. Conversely, 'Breaking Wind' still has relative importance from an older person's standpoint.

Where do they come up with the names of the mascots for the teams in sports? I fully understand Lions, Bears, Tigers, Bulldogs, Eagles, Falcons, Panthers, Wolves, etc. They sound dangerous, tough and fearsome – who would dare show up to play those teams? On the other hand, there are many examples of sports teams with very strange mascots. Here are some examples:

The University of California Irvine "Anteaters".

The UC Santa Barbara "Gauchos".

The UC Santa Cruz "Banana Slugs". Clearly, there must be something in the water in California!

Campbell University "Fighting Camels" – really? Do they intimidate by spitting at you?

Colby College "White Mules" - stubborn maybe, but how about Mustangs instead?

The University of Maryland "Terrapins" – isn't that the same as turtles? Does the name intimate they are slow?

Florida Southern "Moccasins" – will they get walked over?

Idaho "Vandals" – how will they steal the game?

New York University "Violets" – as in shrinking?

North Carolina "Tar Heels" – will they get stuck to the turf?

Oregon "Ducks" – do they waddle down the field?

Trinity Christian College "Trolls" –will they play in the sunlight?

North Carolina School of the Arts "Fighting Pickles" – beware the gherkins?

Shimer College "Flaming Smelts" – sounds fishy, do they really stink?

How and why did someone come up with the word 'O'clock' to describe the time of day? Why is it used only on the hour? You say twelve o'clock, but not four thirty o'clock, right? My grandfather used to say 'half past four' rather than 'four thirty' anyway – or 'quarter of five' instead of 'four forty-five'. This can be rather confusing for people of all ages. Personally, I think some old Irish guy got tired of telling everyone the time of day and started using the expression, "are ye daft man, it's eight o'clock to be sure". Maybe his given name was Shamus O'clock. Maybe he was the 'town crier' who had the job of lighting the gas street lights while yelling, "twelve o'clock and all's well". Good thing he didn't have to deal with daylight savings time! By the way, I think the guy who invented the clock as a time keeping devise was a genius – but how did he know what time it was the first time he set the hands?

There's a TV program currently running, I think on the Sci-Fi channel, called "Mysteries of the Unknown". Doesn't this title seem a little weird? Aren't they sort of one and the same? Almost sounds like a double negative. If these episodes are really mysteries, and are about the unknown, at the conclusion of the program are they 'known'? It must have taken the producers all of ten seconds to come up with this title. Genius.

Proper English speech often makes no sense. Here's something I've wondered about for a long time. If 'rhetoric' is the art of speaking or writing effectively intending to be persuasive or impressive by using eloquent communication to influence its audience, why does use of a 'rhetorical question' require no answer?   Why even ask the question in the first place if you don't expect a reply?   Maybe some people just like to hear themselves talk! Do you think?

Here are some examples of phrases or expressions (paradoxes) that I don't get:

Why do 'fat chance' and 'slim chance' mean the same thing if fat and slim are opposites?

Don't 'drink and drive'. As a kid, I thought this meant an adult wasn't allowed to drink anything (water, lemonade, coke, etc.) while behind the wheel. Would he or she get electrocuted if they grabbed the steering wheel with wet hands after drinking something?   I didn't realize they were talking about beer or liquor.

Why do we have noses that run and feet that smell?

Why do we park in a driveway and drive on a parkway?

Why are a wise man and a wise guy just the opposite?

How can a house burn up as it burns down?

How can you fill in a form while filling it out?

Why does an alarm go off by going on?

Why is a peanut called a peanut? It's not a pea or a nut.

Why call it eggplant? – there's no egg in it.

Why call it hamburger? – there's no ham in it.

Why call it a pineapple? – it consists of neither pine nor apple.

Why a 'boxing ring'? It's a square! Aren't rings round, like a circle?

Why quicksand? – it takes forever for something to sink in it.

Why call it a guinea pig? – it's neither from Guinea nor is it a pig.

We know vegetarians eat vegetables; does it follow that humanitarians eat humans?

Why do lots of people today use the expression, 'back in the day'? Which day? Don't they mean, 'back in the old days', or 'in a galaxy far, far, away'?

Why do passengers line up thirty to sixty minutes early to board their plane? Don't they realize everyone will land at the same time?

Shouldn't the people who created all of the words, phrases, and language rules concerning English speech be confined to an asylum for the verbally insane?

Why is there so much cussing, swearing and general cursing in most of the movies made today? Is it necessary? Does it really reflect reality? What's the point and what does it add to the film? Does it make the film more believable? Do movie goers demand it of producers and script writers? I doubt it. I cringe whenever I hear it. I don't talk that way with my friends and family, so I should pay money to hear it in a theatre? Don't the people who review the films for rating purposes get tired of hearing the bad language? I'm not endorsing censorship, but I think it adds to the denigration of the industry and limits the age range of the audience. In other words, the use of profanity is potentially reducing revenue and profitability for the film industry today. Strictly from a financial standpoint, it's hurting the industry and reflects poorly on the decision makers in Hollywood. Worst of all, it's giving the wrong message to our society. People go to the movies, hear the language and figure it's alright to act that way themselves. Maybe it's sort of self-perpetuating. I certainly can't compare the Academy Award winning films of yesteryear with those of today. There are many other differences which separate them - one is offensive language.

I personally thought the phrases created by Soupy Sales (a beloved comic of local Detroit television in the 50's) were clever. Among my favorites were, "Be true to your teeth or they'll be false to you" and, "When you go to cross the street, keep your mind on your feet!" Clever - they don't make 'em like they used to!

There are lots of common phrases we use that are redundant, unnecessary, and I just plain don't get. Here are some favorites:

"Do you think so?" – Yes, I do, otherwise I wouldn't have said it.

"Needless to say," or "It goes without saying" or "Having said that" – so why do you have to say this in the first place?

"Can I ask you a question?" – So why not just go ahead and ask it? Actually, I think you just did.

"Can we talk?" – Well, I know I can and since you just did, I guess so!

"It is what it is" – Reminds me of high school geometry (if X=Y and Y=Z, then X=Z or something like that!). Besides, no one said it isn't what it is or is not.

Then there are these additional things I wonder about and also don't get:

Why do we refer to a 'pair' of pants or glasses when there is only one?

Why should you need an appointment to visit a psychic? Shouldn't they already sense that you're coming?

Statistically, if 4 out of 5 people suffer from headaches, does that mean the 5th person enjoys them?

Why do they put Braille dots on the keypad of the drive-up ATM?

Why did Kamikaze pilots wear helmets?

Why do doctors and lawyers call what they do 'practice'?

Where does it mention in the nursery rhyme that Humpty Dumpty was an egg?"

Why does sour cream have an expiration date?

Who shuts the door when the bus driver gets off? How does he get back in?

When you catch a fish and release it, does he tell his friends he was abducted by aliens?

When they say, "Coming to a theatre near you", how do they know where you live?

At what age does it change from 'pretending' to 'lying'?

What happens if you get half scared to death twice?

Is there ever a time when mattresses aren't 'on sale'?

Why don't shorts cost half as much as pants?

Why do they call it a 'hot water heater', you're heating cold water, right?

In like fashion, who came up with the 'oxymoron' as a figure of speech? The first part, 'oxy' comes from the Greek for 'sharp' while the second part, 'moron' is Greek for 'dull'. While listening to a college professor deliver a lecture, Groucho Marx later remarked, "I thought my razor was dull until I heard his speech!" Gives new meaning to being called 'dull' doesn't it? Here are some thought provoking examples which combine opposite meanings:

Jumbo shrimp	Same difference
Seriously funny	Awfully good
Act naturally	Small crowd
Deafening silence	Great depression
Pretty ugly	Least favorite
Once again	Civil War

Is there a difference between a 'bold faced lie' and a regular, ordinary, 'run of the mill' lie? Apparently, there is. Sounds like it might have a connection with a rather distinct facial expression (or a type of font used). There are 'little white lies' which by description, appear to be small, harmless, or inconsequential. The 'bold faced lie' would seem to be the whopper - the granddaddy of them all. The question is, of course, why do people lie in the first place? Is it to enhance self-esteem or appear superior to others? Are lies spoken to cover-up the 'truth'? A fib would seem like stretching the truth - an exaggeration of sorts. I don't know about you, but my Mom always knew when I was fibbing - and it usually resulted in the threat of washing my mouth out with soap!

Why do we pronounce words differently than they are spelled? Like 'marshmellow' rather than marshmallow, or 'duck tape' instead of duct tape? Sometimes mispronunciation involves dialects from different areas of the country. In any case, here are some favorites that drive me nuts:

Jute box (juke box)
Valentime's Day (Valentine's Day)
Liberry (library)
Axe (ask)
Your (You're)
Skedule (Schedule)

Grochery (Grocery)

Excape (Escape)

Expresso (Espresso)

Relator (Realtor)

Would of (Would Have)

Crik (Creek)

In similar fashion, if the plural of foot is feet, then shouldn't boot be beet?   How 'bout if more than one tooth is teeth, then wouldn't booth be beeth? Am I the only person who thinks about these things?

I've often wondered about the difference between and correctness of naming children 'Junior '(Jr) versus 'the second' (II). While usually pertaining to a son, apparently you can use these suffixes for daughters as well, although they would most likely be ridiculed by their peers and possibly become scarred for life – then again, everything goes today. The most common reason for naming a baby after his father or another family member, obviously, is the hope that he will carry on the tradition and/or become like his predecessor.   English Kings and their lineage are great examples – Henry IV, Henry V, and so on. The confusion continues in naming the second in line because it is possible to use either II (the second) or Jr (Junior). Apparently the 'rules' involve using Jr when the child is going to have the exact same name as his father and the father is still living at the time. On the other hand, II is properly used when the child is taking the name of a family member other than his father – like his uncle, grandfather, and so forth. In order to use II, the names must be identical, including the middle name. In summary: Both are used to identify that the person is the second in the family to have the name, Jr is used when the son has the same name as the father, and, II is used when the elder family member is anyone other than the father. Whew! I don't even want to get into surnames!

When does one stop saying 'Happy New Year' when greeting someone after the first of the year? Is there an appropriate cut-off date such as January 8th? By the same token, is there a similar cut-off date to take down your tree, decorations and outdoor holiday lights? I get the fact that it's often too cold to go outside to remove the lights, but how about just switching off the timer. Some people let their lights blaze on for weeks – to the delight of the local electric company. Maybe they are hoping the heat generated from the glowing lights will actually melt the snow. In a similar vein, it's 'Merry Christmas' in the US but 'Happy Christmas' in England. I don't get why there isn't a universally accepted phrase. While sacrificing originality, wouldn't it be simpler?

Look! It's the Statue of Liberty! …

Why do some people hug or kiss when greeting each other while others simply just shake hands? Is it an ethnic thing? Does it come naturally or is it acquired or learned behavior? Personally, I believe it depends on the way you were raised, with a fair amount of ethnicity thrown in. Italians (my wife's lineage) are known to be very warm, more demonstrative, emotional individuals. The English (my ancestors), on the other hand, endeavor to show no emotion whatsoever - think 'stiff upper lip'. They work very hard at it. I'll give you an example of what I mean. When I greet my brother after an absence of, say, two months (who shares my English genes, by the way), we will invariably firmly shake hands. The same was true with my father - always shook hands, never hugged or kissed. If, on the other hand, I happen to run into my wife's Italian relatives (having just seen them the day before), we will routinely hug and kiss. Why does this dichotomy persist? Shouldn't there be a standard, agreed upon method of socially greeting one another? It can be very awkward and sometimes embarrassing as well. If everyone is hugging, do you follow suit? Do you hug and kiss or are they two separate options? How do you know which one is appropriate? Do you lean in from the left or the right? Is there a proper, prescribed, protocol? Do you hug or kiss yet again

33

when you part company? What if you bump heads or noses? Sometimes I've smashed my glasses into theirs. Again, awkward. What if you go for a hug but the other person doesn't reciprocate? Again, embarrassing. The customs and habits of very different cultures are often hard to understand let alone reconcile.

Typical English Behavioral Customs: Most often, the prim and proper Brits simply won't debate with, argue with, or in any manner, confront anyone in public. It just isn't done! They're too polite and honestly can't be rude to anyone (even if it is deserved). It's not inherent in their heritage or DNA makeup. They're even excessively polite with posted road signs involving driving instructions - "Mind your surroundings whilst maneuvering" or appropriate behavior for pet owners - "Please don't allow your dog to foul the footpath". They constantly struggle to avoid conversation with others at all costs, in large part because they can't stand to make small talk. They don't necessarily want to get to know their neighbors or co-workers either. It's not that they're snobby, they just don't want to interfere or bother anyone - they want to be left alone. They resist most social activity due to the awkwardness involved. They're definitely afraid to over stay their welcome and, by the same token, will refuse to tell a guest to leave when it's late and time for them to go home. They don't change facial expression much - they certainly don't smile very often (perhaps embarrassed by their bad teeth). 'Tipping' the waitstaff in a restaurant is not expected - they feel it's unnecessary, excessive and even vulgar. By contrast, they feel Americans give away money to everyone all the time - "Look, she's giving yet another tip to that other person as well!" They don't make a scene or cause a ruckus of any sort. They follow orders extremely well and like to be told what to do - it gives them a sense of order and maintains decorum. Generally, the men have very few close friends (mates). Sometimes men (particularly in Scotland) will wear kilts in public and think nothing of it! Even the Royal Family will do so themselves on certain special occasions. How can you possibly have a serious conversation with someone while staring at his kilt – especially if it happens to be a windy day? They take a lovely 'Holiday' not a vacation. When they do go, it's usually to the same place, year after year - and it invariably rains the entire time. It is, however, much more important to have bad weather back home than good weather while on Holiday. That way you can feel guilty pleasure! Remember, they have, on average, only 60 sunny days out of 365 in England. They make Holiday plans a year in advance and invariably always over-prepare for the trip. They pack clothes for every possible weather condition and bring along some English food (they reason you can't get familiar or proper 'good food' anywhere outside the UK). They have a horrible fear of using foreign toilets coupled with the phobia of having no paper in the stall. They also dislike haggling over the price of souvenirs - the Brits will just 'grin and bear it' rather than make a fuss. They find it difficult to wish 'Merry Christmas' to people on the street because, as mentioned earlier, they don't like to talk to strangers. They fear the check-out line at the grocery and just want to 'get on with it'. Most are even too modest to accept a compliment. They are, indeed, a very private and reserved bunch of people. That is, until they hit their local pub, or attend a football match - then all 'Hell' breaks loose! It's only under these circumstances they will 'let loose, go crazy' and sing, dance, yell, scream, cavort, and even show affection in public! I must give proper credit to the 2015 Netflix series "Very British Problems" for sharing many of the above observations about the British population – it's spot on (good show - well done, then)!

Typical Italian Behavioral Customs: Italians share few, if any, of these English characteristics. Their behavior is quite the opposite. They are often warm, outgoing, engaging, expressive, and flamboyant. One drawback is they sometimes can be rather loud and assertive. My dear wife is Italian (actually, Sicilian) so I've witnessed many of these customs and traits first hand. Speaking of hands, I'm often amazed that many Italians wildly wave their hands and arms while talking. I've also heard they bite their hands while gesturing and speaking. Plus, if you see them moving their hand from side to side in the proximity of their throat, you should know that death is eminent! If they found themselves 'bound and gagged' I'll wager they would still find a way to talk! My father-in-law once joked that he was going to measure my feet for cement shoes which made me laugh - nervously. I first met many of her relatives at a family funeral. The emotional weeping and wailing were almost unbelievable and certainly shocking to me. One woman was actually draped over the open casket while sobbing. Suffice it to say, I wasn't ready for this type of dramatic display - my wife had not prepared me. Apparently, she thought this was 'normal' behavior. Her relatives must have thought, "What's wrong with him, he's not even crying!" What did they expect from me, I never even knew the deceased person. While there, I was introduced to a beloved uncle who, rather oddly I noticed, had hair growing right out of his knuckles - something I had never quite seen before (unless you count Lon Chaney Jr. in 'The Wolfman'). As I attempted to offer my condolences, he interrupted me by asking, "Hey, how mucha you make?" I didn't know how to respond. Scenes from 'The Godfather' flashed before my eyes. I began to look around the room for Luca Brasi or Sal Tessio lurking in the shadows while planning my escape strategy. Later my wife explained, "He meant well". A kind expression I would continue to hear for years to come and understand.

Like all ethnic groups, the Italians also have their own specialty foods. My mother-in-law routinely made home-made bread, pasta, sauce, soup, and other favorite dishes for her family, which they treasured and loved. My personal experience with spaghetti sauce had been limited mostly to Chef Boy-ar-dee - right out of the can. I had no idea that each Italian homemaker created her unique sauce with a secret recipe which gave it a distinctive flavor. She literally 'slaved over a hot stove' all day on Saturday to prepare the Sunday family meal. When I first tasted my future mother-in-law's sauce at a family dinner, I was asked to comment on the quality of the sauce. Suddenly, I felt as though I was in an old E. F. Hutton commercial. There was dead silence, everyone was straining to hear my reply - you could have heard a pin drop. Not knowing my response would impact my future relationship with the entire family, I simply said, "It's OK". No one said a word. I certainly didn't intend to hurt her feelings, I simply didn't realize how important this was to her and the family. Years later, we laughed about it, but at the time it must have gone over like a lead balloon. Another funny thing is they never leave the table. They just sit there, eating nuts, until the next meal! Then there was the first Thanksgiving dinner at her aunt's house (and my first exposure to the famous legend of the 'chicken feet soup'). Holiday meals were served in delicious courses - first came the home-made soup, followed by salad, pasta, entree, more pasta, and several more entrees before desert, cookies and more sweets - all painstakingly hand made. Whew! It was an eating marathon. My wife's Aunt, who was hosting, had a huge pot of chicken soup boiling in the kitchen. As I was complimenting her on how wonderful the soup smelled, she told us her secret, explaining that she had used actual chicken feet, chopped off at the ankles, to flavor the soup (as called for in the traditional recipe). I had never heard of soup being made this way. The only chicken feet I had ever seen were still attached to the leg! I needed smelling salts to revive me while sprawled on the floor! All experiences considered however, the Italian people are a very warm, inviting, close knit, and endearing group. I've come to love and admire her entire family very much!

I believe the first thing we Americans did after the revolution was to purposely start driving on the opposite side of the road from the Brits. Maybe it was our way of boldly demonstrating our independence and rubbing it in (confusing and driving them nuts). Actually, I stubbornly feel it's 'they' who drive on the wrong side, not us. Perhaps it was just our way of sharing the road as there were still some Brits living here with us. The question is, why did they stay? I would have caught the first frigate home. English food can have very strange names as well. Couldn't they come up with a better name for 'clotted cream'? Blood clots, and cream curdles. How about thickened cream or really soft butter, instead? Much more appetizing, right? Then there's 'gentleman's paste' - a disgusting anchovy-based spread or relish. If women have never tasted it, they're not missing anything! Don't even get me started on 'deviled kidneys' or 'smoked kippers', Mr. Porky Scratchlings, 'pickled pig's feet', 'cucumber sandwiches' or the old standby, Marmait! On the other hand, enjoying a formal afternoon 'High Tea' is a very memorable, delightful dining experience and, 'to die for'!

In a more humorous sense, the politest people are the British as far as saying, "I'm sorry". In truth, I'm not sure it's a matter of politeness or just inbred modesty, temerity, and paranoia. They seem to use the word 'sorry' multiple times in a span of about two minutes. "Sorry 'bout that", "Sorry, can I just squeeze past?", "Sorry, I was in this queue (line) first", "Sorry, would you please pass me the malt vinegar?", "Sorry, I'm going to have to ask you to leave", "Sorry to disturb", "Sorry, what?", and the most incredulous, "Sorry, I'm sorry you feel that way!" They may be some of the 'sorriest' people I've ever met. Why are they so 'bloody sorry' - they didn't do anything wrong? It's not their fault!

Have you ever noticed that most Canadians don't say or use the word 'the' before a noun? It's true. I live very close to the US - Canadian border, so I grew up hearing it a lot – still do. As an example, you and I might say, "They had to take her to the hospital." They, on the other hand, would report, "They had to take her to hospital." - completely omitting the word 'the'. Listen to a Canadian news station and you'll hear what I mean. 'The' is the most used grammatical article in English speech and the only definite article. Does this happen in other bordering countries that share the same language? Is it only with certain nouns? In a hockey game, the Canadian announcer might say, "Now then Leafs (as in Toronto Maple Leaf's team) bring the puck out of their own zone". Why not "...the Leafs"? In a similar fashion, many Brits constantly finish a sentence with the word 'then'. Like, "I'm going to go warm up the car, then", or "I'll see you a bit later, then". Alternatively, they're also known to complete their sentence with the word 'what' (pronounced whot). "You're looking rather chipper, what"? or "That's a fancy pair of trousers, what"? I don't get it!

What's the deal with parents naming their child after a former family member? Not all practice this custom, so It must have to do with cultural tradition. In my English family history, there were multiple Georges', Charles', and Williams'. In my wife's Italian family, the first-born son was always named after the father's father (which I believe is the same as his paternal grandfather). Thus, you might end up with several people with the same name in the same room at the same time! How 'bout some originality and breaking with tradition? The most extreme example that comes to mind is George Foreman who named all five of his sons George. How can they not have whiplash when someone says, "Hey George"?

Are you gonna eat that? ...

What's the preoccupation with over-eating in our country? How did it start and how can we stop it? There's an old expression – 'Do you eat to live or live to eat?'. There's no question that obesity is shortening lives and has become an epidemic. Almost everyone has been or is currently on a diet to lose weight. While many are trying to become more health conscious, we still have some, including young children, struggling with their weight. I remember in the 1950's fast food places and 'all-you-can-eat' buffets became popular. They called them 'smorgasbords' which I think is Danish or Swedish for a never ending, unlimited supply of buffet style food. My brothers and I used to refer to them as 'pig troughs'. The obvious attraction was that for one price, you could go back time and again for second and third helpings. What a deal! Not the healthiest food you could eat, but at the time, who cared – you were getting a lot for your money. At least I think that was behind the thinking. Most of our folks or grandparents experienced food rationing during the Great Depression of the 1930's or the Second World War. Many others simply went without food for days on end. After the war, people had more disposable income (money) and they wanted 'value' for their dollars. They remembered the recent past and never wanted to

43

go hungry again.   It became 'fun' to take the family out to a restaurant or 'carry-out' food to bring home.   I think overindulgence also crept in when the 'bulk food' stores arrived on the scene.   It became too easy to buy more than you really needed. 'Free samples' further encouraged patrons to over eat and made you feel you were getting free food.   If they timed it right, senior citizens and college kids could eat free all day long at Sam's Club or Costco without buying anything!

My folks enjoyed having Chinese food every once in a while. Most often it was taken out, but, on occasion, we dined in the restaurant.   Don't you love the uniqueness of most Chinese restaurants? Think about it. They all have pretty much the same layout, décor, and, look – usually no side wall windows.   The entire staff are always very friendly and accommodating.   They are also usually all related to each other.   I never asked, but I think most employees were from the same nuclear and extended family. Setting aside the customers, have you ever seen a non-Asian in the building?   Your waitress is always in a hurry to provide fast, courteous service.   Your place mat told you what animal represented you in their zodiac – like if you were born in 1945, you were born in the year of the pig, or ox, or whatever. I don't recall any flattering animals involved with this deal.   You had a choice of mostly the same food – either Mandarin or Cantonese, and of course it was delicious and exactly what you had come to expect. Last but not least, you always got a fortune cookie with a special message inside at the end of the meal. I don't know how they avoid burning up the paper message during the baking process. Last week, my fortune message read, "Find a peaceful place where you can make plans for the future". I told my granddaughter I thought it would be a coffin. She just rolled her eyes. The food is often very reasonably priced and you get a lot to eat. So reasonable that if you had a $10 coupon or gift card, you and your wife could eat dinner, take half home for a future meal, and make a profit on the whole deal! Speaking of asking for a box to take home leftovers, which is the proper top and which is the bottom? – they look the same to me and they're never clearly marked. Usually I get the 50/50 chance wrong and end up with it leaking all over the seat or carpeting in the car. Sometimes I even leave the restaurant forgetting to take the dumb box with me. Sort of defeats the whole purpose, doesn't it?

I noticed the other day that some food and beverages we have in our pantry and refrigerator are clearly beyond their expiration dates. I'm sure that goes for a couple of the meds we take as well. These 'labels' typically read, 'sell by' or 'best if used by' or 'discard after'. Does the average older person actually look at the dates and routinely throw out the stuff that has expired? I doubt it. Does the CDC keep track of the number of people who have died from taking expired drugs and painkillers? Does the coroner check this in determining cause of death? Probably not. How do they even know the correct date to put on this stuff in the first place? Isn't aging only really important if you're talking about cheese or wine? Young people probably are, I'm sure, more aware of this than us older folk. My theory is that older people tend to disregard the expiration dates more often, maybe because of the cost involved in replacing something they feel is still 'perfectly good'. It may also be akin to the '5 second rule' – that is, if food is retrieved from the floor in a timely fashion, it's ok to consume. Or, it could simply be a matter of needing to make an appointment with an optometrist and replace their glasses – but that's an expensive proposition as well. Not a good thing if you can't see. Oh well, as someone once said, "Enjoy Life! - It has an expiration date!"

Before these cautionary expiration warning dates appeared on food and beverage containers, my Mom would give it her 'nose test'. "Here, let me smell 'of it'", she would say, and then pronounce it edible or not. How reassuring! If she deemed the food suitable to continue eating, she would then follow up with, "We'd better use it up". What, before it goes 'down'? Probably meaning down the drain. My dear Aunt Pauline would often say, "It's still goooood". How did she know without smelling 'of it'? Some women just have a sixth sense about food poisoning, I guess. All I know is none of us kids ever died from eating food gone bad, thankfully. Let's face it, expiration dates are definitely confusing. Do you go by the 'use by' date or by the 'sell by' date? It always reminds me of being in high school chemistry class and having to memorize the half-life (is this the same as shelf life?) of plutonium or whatever. Like you'll ever find that information useful in real life! Anyway, all you have to do if you have any doubt is just have an elderly woman 'smell of it'!

While we're still on the gruesome topic of food causing death, what was all the concern about waiting an hour before going swimming after eating when we were kids? Who came up with that maxim? I don't know, but every mom adhered to it religiously. All I do know, is that I lost a lot of good pool time over the years and never knew a kid who got a stomach cramp and croaked in the pool. "Look, is that Ralphie floating face down over there?" "Yeh, but I don't think he's really drowning, he just wolfed down three hot dogs and didn't wait an hour before swimming." All the Moms would be smiling knowingly - without actually saying, "I told you so!"

I just finished watching the annual Nathan's Famous Hot Dog eating contest held at Coney Island every 4th of July. Eleven-time champion Joey Chestnut downed 74 'dogs', including the buns of course, in 10 minutes. He retains 'The Mustard Belt' and world title. Pie eating contests at county fairs are equally intriguing. Then there are cherry pit spitting contests, plunger throwing, log tossing, log splitting, tree climbing, greased pig chasing, and, the Scandinavian rock throwing challenge, among others. Why do people enter these contests? Isn't it embarrassing? Have they no shame? Personally, I think they probably don't have spouses to prevent them from jumping in. Think about it. Your name will be added to the Guinness Word Book of records and you'll undoubtedly go down in history. Oh, the publicity, renown, and fame involved! You'd be an instant celebrity on Facebook or Twitter. You might even be invited to appear on the 'Late Show'. It would be like hitting the game winning home run in the bottom of the ninth in the 7th game of the World Series. The only drawback with the Nathan's contest, as I see it, would be the sight of your fellow competitors 'tossing their cookies', or, in this case, 'dogs', live on national television.

Why is it often so difficult to peel a hard-boiled egg without destroying half of the egg in the process? Everyone has their own special 'patented' method of boiling eggs, right? Leave them in the boiling pan for a certain length of time, immerse them immediately into cold water after boiling, use baking soda, etc. Even then, there's no consistency. Nothing seems to work 100% of the time. I guess I should ask and rely on cooks who consistently make great 'deviled eggs' because they always turn out perfect!

Turning to hamburgers, let's talk a bit about the Big Boy Restaurants and their famous 'double-decker' burger. Legend has it that in 1936, Bob Wian sold his DeSoto convertible to purchase a small hamburger stand in Glendale, California. He named it Bob's Pantry. One night in 1937, a regular customer requested something different, not on the menu. Bob created the first 'double-decker' hamburger. It was an instant success. One fan of the new burger was a chubby six-year old boy in sagging overalls. Apparently, he offered to sweep up in exchange for a free burger (must have been related to 'Wimpy' of Popeye fame). In honor of his young friend, Wian decided to name his new hamburger the 'Big Boy'. Along the way, a comic book called The Adventures of Big Boy was born. The Big Boy character was originated by yet another patron who sketched the original icon one day on a paper napkin. This comic was co-written by Stan Lee of Marvel Comics fame until about 1961. What I don't get is why the character 'Big Boy' never had a real name! He had a girl friend named Dolly and a dog named Nugget, but to this day he remains nameless!

Have you noticed that the people who conduct today's research and interpret recent studies now indicate its fine to have two to three cups of regular (caffeinated) coffee each day. These are the same people who told us awhile back to stay away from caffeine at all costs! By the way, what's the deal with 'free grazing' cattle and 'cage free' or 'free range' chickens? Do the cattle and/or chickens really know (or care) where they are at any given time? They're still too dumb to come in out of the rain! Have they demanded this freedom from their owners and union representatives? Are the sheep grazing ranchers going to cause a 'ruckus' over this like back in the 1880's?   What about the horses and other barnyard creatures – are they going to be compensated for the loss of their portion of the pasture? Will we have a shortage of decent grass for them to munch on? Before you know it, they will all refuse to come back into the barn at the end of the day.   The barn won't be good enough for them! They'll be demanding a 'ranch' condo and special 'posh' food – fancy that! There's no telling where this will all end.

Why do seniors seem to pass more gas as they get older? In reality, it actually has to do with poor fitting dentures, diet, and eating too fast. Honestly. Gases produced during the digestion process include hydrogen, oxygen, nitrogen, carbon dioxide and methane – the last one being the stinky one. Sounds to me like you don't want to be anywhere near an open flame when you (or an older friend) let one rip. It certainly gives added meaning to the expression 'the greenhouse effect'. Also, "Honey, I'm going to run out and gas up the car" can literally be taken two ways! Interestingly, as a side note, pumpernickel (as in bread) is a German word meaning 'goblin that breaks wind.' I suppose older people could regularly take an anti-flatulent such as Gas-X. They will know what that is because the law requires that there be language on the bottle stating that flatulence is "referred to as gas' (as if the name of the product wouldn't give it away!). There's even a TV commercial running which shows an animated bed mattress complaining about the occupants always 'gassing up' the sheets. Some people take 'Beano' before a meal to ward off the gas attack. What I don't get is what's happening inside your digestive tract after you take it. Doesn't the gas eventually have to come out somewhere, somehow, sometime? Won't you eventually explode or simply float away into outer space? "Hey, is that the Goodyear Blimp passing overhead? No wait, I believe it's Floyd - he must have taken too much Gas-X last night!" All I know for sure is that more and more things in my shopping cart are for 'fast relief'. I think part of the problem revolves around the fact that seniors can't hear or smell very well, so they're unaware they are even farting. Maybe they are aware and are just marking their territory. Most often, it shouldn't really present a problem as there's usually no one to offend around the house. Even if your wife or pet are home, they are probably already used to it, so feel free to let it fly! A good idea is to spray extra strength Febreze on your pants every once in a while. The writing on the Febreze bottle claims to "eliminate tough odors in fabrics for lasting freshness". Sounds like that should do the trick. Or, if the lingering smell really does bother you and is too much for others to bear as well, you could simply throw them in the wash (this, of course, assumes that you have another pair of clean trousers to wear that fit!).

My wife and I visited a restaurant with friends recently while in Florida. It was located on a small island and everything on it looked like it was frozen in the fifties. From the delightful little colorfully painted trailers and mobile homes to the little restaurant constructed, in part, from the hull of an old wooden ship, the entire island was a pleasant trip back in time. The waitress gave us a tour of the dining rooms, explaining the history involved. Other friends who had eaten there previously gave it high marks for lunch. The place lived up to its reputation – the food was very good, the service was excellent, and the atmosphere was pure rustic Americana with a nautical twist. We even had a nice view of the marina and docks. When the hostess seated us, we noticed there were no menus on the table. It wasn't very long before she dragged over two large triangular shaped easels. Next, she carried over two huge (2 feet by 3 feet) cardboard menus and placed them on the easels. I thought this was pretty peculiar until I looked around the dining room and saw the same set-up at all the tables. How nice, I thought, until I realized all the patrons were older people, like us - and then it all made perfect sense. Easy to read, so we all put away our bifocals.

The other day, my wife decided to look up a recipe for au gratin potatoes. In this fancy chef's book, which cost an arm and a leg, she found one that read, 'prepare one package au gratin potatoes as directed'. I don't get it! Did I really need to purchase this expensive book to tell me to go to the market and buy a package of prepared mix?   The directions are on the package anyway!

Restaurants in our town generally give you way too much food to eat.   I think somewhere along the line, Americans began demanding larger and larger portions of food when they dined out – no doubt wanting more for their money and not seeing the obesity crisis around the corner.   Probably another example of 'depression era' philosophy along with 'more is better'.   Most of us, at one time or another, have asked for a take home or carry out box when we can't finish our meal and want to enjoy the leftovers later at home.   These 'doggie bags' have always been confusing to me (not just because we have no intention of giving it to the dog or don't even have a dog).   Specifically, I can never differentiate between the top and the bottom of the box.   More than once, food has leaked out because I had it upside down.   I can't tell you how many times I've left it at the restaurant.   Upon returning two minutes later, I find that they have already thrown it away (much faster than the service you received when they brought it to your table in the first place!).   Other times, I've opened the box at home a day or two later to find someone else's food.   To be on the safe side, I guess I should write my name on it.   With my luck, the waitress has already disappeared with the only pen in the joint.

While driving home from Florida this past winter, we stopped to eat dinner at a rural restaurant. It's been a local favorite for years and it's obvious that as its popularity grew, they expanded (as did the waste-lines of their patrons) several times. Needless to say, the current floor plan is different than you would expect. The 'down home' menu features hush puppies, pulled pork, smoked pork ribs, and more, with several kinds of BBQ sauce to choose from. While we were there, large families were flocking in every few minutes. The owner clearly owns a 'gold mine' – people were literally beating down his door to get in. The funny thing is, when you enter this place, there is an old-fashioned scale conveniently located just inside the door. What are you supposed to do, weigh yourself before and after you eat your dinner? I was tempted but didn't hop on to see how much weight I had gained while dining there.

It's in our genes...

I don't understand why there's such a huge difference between a woman going to a salon to get her hair cut (or colored, styled, tinted, highlighted, dyed, etc.) and a man going to the local barbershop for a periodic trim (unless you live in Beverly Hills, California, that is). I'm not just talking about the cost involved, either. For women, it's a big deal - a serious social event with networking repercussions far beyond the actual outing itself. Other women actually notice right away and will converse for hours about it. "Oh Harriett, it makes you look so much younger!" Or, "Sylvia, I'll bet that's so easy to take care of." Or "Let me take a picture to show my stylist." Men don't talk to each other about their haircuts. Can you imagine one guy saying to another, "Hey Dave, really cute haircut - I love it!" If asked, we often don't even remember where we went, let alone the name of the person who cut it. If the truth were known, most of us dread going and just want to get it over with - sort of like the dentist. On the other hand, if you take the car in for new brakes or tires, then you really have something to discuss with the boys!

It seems as my wife and I get older, we 'talk' to each other by telepathy rather than verbal speech. She will look at me, see the expression on my face, and say "No, we're not getting a dog!" or, in response to a different expression, "No (for the hundredth time), we're not buying a condo in Florida!"   It's getting to the point where we only speak audibly when we're arguing with each other!

I recently went to an outdoor evening concert in a city park. Nice venue and very well attended – mostly by older folks. Probably because they featured Big Band music from the 1940's. During intermission, I had to visit the men's bathroom. The line was two blocks long.   Strangely, the corresponding line at the lady's restroom was very short.   This was definitely a phenomenon none of us had ever witnessed before (and a welcomed surprise for the women). The ladies were smiling and waving to the men waiting in line as they sauntered into their bathroom – as if to say, "Now you know how we feel!"   I wondered what could have caused such a reversal in the laws of nature until I figured out it was due to old age prostate issues!

Why are the buttons and zippers on men's garments on the opposite side of women's clothing (and vice versa)?   My wife gave me a fleece jacket to wear once when I was cold and I noticed that the zipper was the opposite of what I was used to. "Hey look, I blurted out, some idiot made it backwards!" Then my wife, who operated a women's dressmaking business after she retired, explained that it wasn't a mistake. Apparently, it's been purposely done that way for centuries. The buttons and zippers on men's clothing are on the opposite side of women's clothes. At first, I didn't understand why the manufacturers would do this. Years ago, it turns out that wealthy women who never dressed themselves (think Queen Elizabeth II or any other monarch) employed lady's maids to help them get into and then out of their clothes. When doing so, the helper faced the person she was dressing. It was more natural and comfortable for the maid to fasten the buttons in a familiar fashion. For some reason it stuck and has remained this way to the present. The only thing (for a guy) worse than his zipper splitting apart half-way up or down, is forgetting to 'zip up' at all after using the bathroom. It's only after hearing your old aunt saying "The horse is out of the barn" or some such embarrassing nonsense, that men pay more attention.

As a retired, married couple, we have three calendars in our house – 'his', 'hers', and 'ours'. You would think the 'ours' calendar would suffice, wouldn't you? Now the 'ours' has been replaced by an erasable 'white board' in the kitchen. Unlike the calendar, this can be reused over and over again. What this all points to is the unescapable fact that we can't remember much of anything anymore. We have to write everything down (or put it in our phones). One exception to this is when the phone rings and it's your doctor's office reminding you of an appointment you made a year ago. Nice of them to remember for you – saved you from having to write it down.

Why do our wives insist we throw out our perfectly good shoes and buy new ones simply because we've had them for twenty years or longer? They still look good and are much more comfortable than a new pair. Besides, our shoes don't really go out of style, do they? Give 'em a good polishing up every month or so and you're good to go. One brown and one black pair should last a long, long, time, right? While we're at it, is the word 'pair' singular, plural, or both?

Another observation I've made involves the size of your wallet. I think the older men get, the thicker our wallets become. We cram more stuff in them because we probably can't remember everything we used to – including our own phone number. That's easily explained because we never call ourselves, so how are we expected to remember it? The irony is the more we carry in our wallets, the harder it is to find something when we need it. Our wives will tell us, "You don't really need all that stuff in there, do you"? Mine is almost as large as the wallet George Costanza carried in his hip pocket on the 'Seinfeld' show. Jerry told him he had a filing cabinet under his butt. Wives have a lot of nerve – just look at all the junk they keep in their purses! Why, I couldn't be expected to find something in my wife's purse if my life depended on it. We also don't want to lose anything, so we put it in our wallet to keep it handy. Once on a long drive to Florida (with my huge wallet in my hip pocket) I started to develop numbness in my right leg.

Then the sciatic nerve pain started to radiate from my waist, down my calf, to my right foot. My lower back was killing me! I started complaining (refusing to slow down, of course) and thought I should start looking for a hospital. My wife put down her knitting and calmly said, "Oh my gosh, don't be silly, just take that ridiculous wallet out of your pocket, you're pinching a nerve and cutting off the blood supply to your leg!" Yep, that did the trick.

I saw on the news recently that the Boy Scouts of America plan to admit girls into their cub scouts program starting next year. Did I miss something here or is there no longer a Girl Scouts organization? General (later elevated to Lord) Robert Stephenson Smyth Baden-Powell founded the scouting movement for BOYS around 1907 in England. One of his many famous quotations was "Scouting is a game for Boys, under the leadership of Boys, under the direction of a Man". In 1910 when girls wanted to be a part of scouting, a parallel organization, 'The Girl Guides' was formed and run by Agnes Baden-Powell, his sister. What I don't get is if a similar organization already exists for girls, why do they, or their parents, want to join in with the boys? It undoubtedly has to do with money and first amendment rights. If this trend continues, they might as well eliminate the word 'Boy' from 'Boy Scouts' altogether. Sir Baden-Powell must be rolling over in his grave. He would undoubtedly commit suicide if not already dead.

How do you go about firing a family member baby sitter or church volunteer when it's clearly not working out? It's a tough one, and demands careful, tactful, diplomacy. It has to be handled delicately because you are still going to see some of these people on a regular basis. I'm sure making the decision to let a sitter or volunteer go causes many sleepless nights and then you have to tell them! It's a difficult situation for you and them. Awkward, to say the least. Text or email is definitely not the appropriate way to do it. It must be face to face. What I don't get is why we worry ourselves to death over it. More often than not, they know it's coming anyway and are ready to move on. If all else fails, you can always have your wife handle this cumbersome task.

Remember the character 'Pat' on Saturday Night Live a few years back? The whole purpose of the sketch was for the viewer to guess whether she was male or female, right? Things have changed so quickly in our society since that time that writers would dare not approach the topic of 'trans-gender' lifestyle in that manner. You can no longer discern a person's gender by their appearance, hair style, or the way they dress or speak. USA Today recently ran an article confirming that New York City has approved and signed into law a gender-neutral option on birth certificates for residents who don't identify as male or female. It's called 'X'. People over the age of 18 can alter their birth certificates to 'X' to reflect their gender choice. For that matter, new Yorkers can change their gender to M, F, or X. Anything goes – and it's OK, and now it's legal. Apparently, parents can choose 'X' for their children from the start and let them decide later in life who they are. Don't these parents run the risk of having their children confused from the beginning? Despite all the sensationalism and prejudice out there, I believe it's OK to accept and love people for who they are, and it's the right thing to do. I'm not endorsing, condoning, or encouraging gay or lesbian sexual behavior, or trying to upset the LGBTQ community here, but, rather, trying not to be judgmental. I strive daily to live by God's second great commandment; to love all of your fellow human beings.

But it's not 'politically correct'...

The most recent 'midterm elections' are finally over. You don't have to keep track of when they take place, all you have to do is turn on your television. All the incumbent politicians as well as the 'wanna-bees' are already using their campaign funds to sponsor their ads – over and over, ad nauseam. There are two things I don't get here. One, who, in their right mind, would really want this job. Secondly, at the end of each and every commercial, the candidate states, "I approve this message". Of course, they do! They just told you, themselves, what they would do if elected! It wasn't someone else speaking on their behalf. If they didn't approve what they just said, wouldn't they be lying? Really - do you think?

Have you noticed lately that almost no one apologizes or says they're sorry in a situation when the occasion clearly calls for it? I honestly think a lot of the anger and 'road rage' we witness today could be avoided by a simple, "I'm sorry" spoken with sincerity. To say "I'm sorry" really takes courage. It diffuses anger and makes the situation much calmer, plus it's just the right thing to do. Maybe people haven't been raised to admit they were wrong and offer an apology. Maybe, in the heat of the moment, they forget to. Maybe they are ashamed or feel if they

63

say 'I'm sorry' it is a sign of weakness, or means they're admitting guilt. Time Magazine recently reported the results of a study by the magazine 'Frontiers in Psychology' where more than 1,000 people said they felt more hurt about a rejection when it contained an apology and that the word sorry made them feel obliged to offer forgiveness when they didn't want to. In my career, I dealt with the public a great deal. Many times, I spoke with someone who felt they had been wronged or something had been handled unfairly, inappropriately, or incorrectly. Usually the first words out of my mouth were an apology – not always to acknowledge they were right and we were wrong (to take the blame), but because I simply felt bad that they felt bad. More often than not, it made the situation calmer. Sometimes they felt better after they had a chance to vent their feelings and have someone listen to and acknowledge their concerns. My Grandmother used to say "Always tell the truth and always apologize when you are wrong". I always knew she was right – saying you're sorry and forgiveness should go hand in hand (it sure would reduce the number of cases pending in our courts, wouldn't it!).

Where is the Highway Patrol when you really need them? Whatever happened to making a 'citizen's arrest' – "Your Honor, there was no police officer nearby, so I did my civic duty and hauled him into court by myself"? Yea, right! You'd get punched out or have your britches sued off of you. I attribute this selfish behavior to being trapped in what I refer to as our 'me first' society. Lots of people apparently feel they are entitled to or have a right to be first. They get irritated or upset when they have to wait their turn or are prevented from exercising the special privilege, they think they have somehow 'earned'. Just wait until they find out about that old biblical expression "...and the first shall be last".

What's the deal with all of the references in the Bible talking about right being better or preferable to left? "Cast your net on the right side...", "He sits at the right hand of God", "Put your sheep on the right, goats on the left', etc. How do we think that makes left-handed individuals feel (let alone all the goats)? Has this resulted in left-handed prejudice? Like they get 'left out', or are given a 'left-handed compliment'. Just curious, I guess. Try sitting next to a left-handed individual at dinner. Anyway, I'm certain all of us guys know we belong on the left because women are always right!

Some Fraternal Organizations are still puzzling to me. It seems several lodges, secret societies, and fraternal orders were named after animals. Here are a few real examples (feel free to look 'em up on Wikipedia or whatever):

Royal Order of Buffaloes. (Do they wear buffalo or bison horned head dresses at their meetings? – I'm sure the distinction is an important part of their ritual)

Friends of Eagles. (Are their members on a separate endangered species list?)

Loyal Order of Moose. (Or LOOM for short, consists of lodges where members meet to conduct philanthropic business. Baseball player, Bill 'Moose" Skowron was a notable member living in Chicago. By 1966, the Lutheran Church forbade membership in the organization – maybe they knew something we don't).

Other 'animal lodges' include The Elks Club, The Lions Club, The Fraternal Order of Owls, The Fraternal Order of Orioles, The Honorable Order of the Blue Goose (for real) and, the Knights of Pythias (OK, not an animal – actually a man's surname).

In addition, there also exists, The Ancient Order of Hibernians. Do they hold meetings during the winter months or are they all asleep till spring? (Oh wait, that's hibernation, sorry).

The Ancient Mystic Order of Samaritans must surely harbor an admired bunch of 'good deed doers'- a phrase coined by that famous wizard behind the curtain.

The Grand Order of Oddfellows (known as the GOOFS for short, has benefited many causes and charities both here and in England. In fact, my grandfather was a member for many years).

66

The Native Sons of the Golden West, not to be out done by or confused with the Sons of the Desert – both being real organizations, but the latter based on a wonderful Laurel and Hardy film.

Now we come to one of my personal favorites, The Improved Order of Red Men. The highest-ranking officer was called 'Great Keeper of the Wampum', and outsiders were referred to as 'pale faces'. Until 1974 the order was open to white members only (really!) and prior to that, in 1904, an off-shoot group emerged called the Afro-American Order of Red Men (unbelievable! – I'm guessing probably defunct today). Notable members of the original group included Theodore and Franklin Roosevelt! How and why did they find time to join up with this bunch? Like I said, you could look it up.

I still wonder about the tradition of placing 'grave blankets' on the graves of someone dear to you, typically during the winter months. I understand it's a somewhat religious ritual of respect and consideration for your departed loved one. Usually made from evergreen boughs with seasonal red bows or ribbons and pine cones attached, they are really quite attractive. They also liven up what would normally be a rather dreary landscape from November through March. The tradition began in the upper Midwest in the United States brought in by the Scandinavians. What I don't get is do you really think you are keeping them warm during the cold winter months? They're not sleeping, they're dead after all, and don't really need a blanket to keep warm! The other thing is that if you believe in an afterlife (don't they mean after death?), and you strongly feel your relative has made it safely to the other side, they aren't really there anyway and don't need the comfort of a blanket.   This is probably a tradition which will be short lived in today's society (Yah, Sure, by Jiminy!).   Why not just post something nice and reassuring on Facebook instead?

That can't be right ...

I've seen billboards (while driving to Florida) that advertise **"CREMATIONS, STARTING AT $500"**. I assume these ads are from local, 'cut rate' funeral homes. Are they attempting to appeal to little people (dwarfs)? Is it only from the waist up or the waist down? Personally, I would be willing to pay extra for the whole deal. What criteria did thy use to arrive at that price? Apparently, this is a southern phenomenon because I haven't seen anything like it up here in the north. Must be something akin to 'boiled peanuts'. UPDATE: A more recent billboard now advertises 'Low cost funerals - Simple cremations only $895'. Must be the effect of inflation. My question would be, what's involved in a more 'complex cremation' and how much does that cost!?

Still another billboard reads **"VASECTOMIES, NEXT EXIT"**. What the heck kind of medical procedure is that?? Is it like driving into an auto lube shop, waiting for a ten-minute oil change, and then pulling back onto the highway? Will your insurance even help cover it? Talk about convenience!

Here's a relatively new billboard I saw in Alabama. This is one of my favorites. Displaying the picture of a dog (I guess in case you forgot what one looks like), the caption reads, **"FIX YOUR PET FOR $5 – FREE RABIES SHOT WITH SURGERY"**. For real! How hard up are these people for business? I imagine every dog within a 50-mile radius 'high tailing it' for the nearest hills. Shouldn't the dog have a say in this matter – doesn't he or she have rights in today's society? It certainly can't be a casual, spur of the moment, decision for the dog! After all, there's no going back on this deal. Rather than crassly pasting the message on a billboard for all to see, surely this must require a rather sensitive face to face discussion first, right? Are they suggesting some weird medical connection between canine infertility and contracting rabies? Does this rationale carry beyond pets to, dare I say it, humans? And while we're at it, don't you feel, as I do, that the $5 price tag cheapens the whole process/experience? I get the fact that many people are always looking for a bargain, but how does the dog feel about it? Give me a break.

Yet another billboard ad from a funeral home in a rural area shows actual photos of the four morticians employed there with 'LFD' typed below their faces. At first, I thought about "Mayberry RFD" but then realized it stood for 'licensed funeral director'. Wow, does that mean there are still un-licensed shops out there? How could all of our government agencies have missed them? Better 'LFD' than 'FBN' (which stands for 'fly by night')! Plus, with their gigantic faces plastered up there, are they saying they want to get to know you ahead of time? Should we 'like them' on Facebook? Who wants to be friends with their embalmer?

While driving through a popular city in Florida, I saw a clever message on a yet another billboard which read, **"IS THE FORCE NO LONGER WITH YOU? – UROLOGY CLINIC AHEAD"**. Again, for real! Now clearly, the advertising firm's executives were big fans of "Star Wars". Does the list of doctors on staff include Vader, Jaba, Anakin, Yoda, Rey, Solo, and Chewbacca? The subtle message is obviously directed at aging males. Having said that, do you really feel eager to pay them a visit? Gee, I want a doctor with a great sense of humor to perform my next prostate exam!

Come to think of it, I do see more and more billboards advertising how to deal with death as you drive closer to Florida. Most are paid for by funeral directors and churches - yep, that about covers it for all us 'snowbirds'! You definitely have our attention! The latest scheme seems to be constructing two billboards, one directly on top of the other. In the first such arrangement I noticed, the top ad is from a local liquor store and the one below is from a local law firm offering assistance with auto accident liability. Get the connection? Another one from a local hotel advertised 'stay with us and eat a free breakfast' - complete with pictures of pancakes, waffles, sausage and bacon, etc. The one underneath was from a diet center offering to help you lose weight! Now, I'm no judge of horse flesh, but does anyone but me think these ads are at cross purposes? I'm not making this up - you could ask my wife!

Whatever became of the old Burma-Shave signs along the side of the road? They were popular during the early years of highway travel. The jingles were very creative, weren't they? I remember asking my Dad to slow down so we could read them – especially the punch line. How did they decide which heavy traffic roads to use? How much did they pay the landowner for the right to put them up? I'll bet the original signs would be worth a lot of money to the right collector today. You can still buy Burma-Shave on Amazon today! Here are some examples of hundreds of their advertising jingles which ran from 1927-1963:

In Cupid's little
Bag of tricks
Here's the one
That Clicks
With Chicks
   - **Burma-Shave**

To Kiss
A Mug
That's like a cactus
Takes more nerve
Than it does practice
- **Burma-Shave**

Dinah doesn't
Treat him right
But if he'd
Shave
Dyna-mite!
- **Burma-Shave**

My job is
Keeping faces clean
And nobody knows
De Stubble
I've seen
- **Burma-Shave**

I went to the local laundromat in town recently. A prominent sign read: Automatic washing machines – Please remove all your clothes when the light goes out. Really? Do the police know about this place?

As we get older, some of us apparently like to visit second hand shops. I saw a sign in one that read, "We will exchange anything – bicycles, furniture, appliances, etc.   Bring your husband along and get a wonderful bargain!"   Two-way interpretation here. They had to be kidding, right?

As you enter a small, nearby rural town there is a sign which reads, 'Welcome to Fredonia, a small town. Population 105.' I'm not making this up! First of all, why do you have to tell everyone it's a small town, isn't it self-evident?   Secondly, is it accurate, and how often do they have to change the sign due to births, deaths, and people just plain leaving - weekly, monthly, yearly? Who's in charge of this sign?   Do they go around and actually count all the residents each morning?   Better yet, who really cares?

Here's something I truly don't get.   This seems totally unnecessary to me.   A road sign reads, 'Do Not Pass while approaching traffic is present'.   Does this make absolutely no sense, or what? Unless you are a blind person (or drunk), why would you attempt to pass a car ahead of you when there are cars zooming by you on the opposing side of the street? Here's another one.   'Prison Area - Do Not Pick Up HITCH-HIKERS'. Do we really have to be warned not to stop and pick up or chat with a stranger on the side of the road here? How about 'State Mental Hospital - Use Caution'.   Only another lunatic would knowingly ask for directions or strike up a conversation with someone in the vicinity.

Local sheriff's departments and police stations still display pictures of their most wanted fugitives. Why didn't they keep them locked up when they took their pictures? Some of these criminals have probably been on the run for years. Shouldn't their photos be updated through an artist's rendering or something? Otherwise, they'll never be recognized and recaptured.

Great headline in our local weekly paper – 'Man kills himself before shooting wife and daughter'. That's quite a feat. Doesn't anyone prove-read the stuff today before they print it?

Here's yet another newspaper quote. "If this strike isn't settled quickly, it may last awhile". Was this written by a relative of Yogi Berra?

Ok, I promise, this is the last one. 'Red tape holds up new bridge. Is this yet another use for good 'ole duct tape?

Travel at your own risk …

A couple of years ago my wife and I were driving south on I-75 in Tennessee. Just outside Knoxville, there had been a very recent and serious rockslide, making most of the lanes impassable. They had to completely close the entire south-bound highway and detour traffic for about 20 miles. We crawled along this little two- lane asphalt road for hours. I quickly realized we were in a rustic wilderness which closely resembled 'Dog Patch, USA'. There were no towns or villages anywhere - no cell phone service, restaurants, gas stations, or bathrooms. I soon became desperate - my back teeth were almost under water, so to speak. Finally, I spotted an old, dilapidated barn off the road and headed for it. My wife said, "What on earth are you doing?" "I really have to go and can't wait any longer, besides, no one will see me for miles out here", I replied. So, I'm relieving myself, standing in mud up to my ankles, behind the cover of this barn, and I look around at the rural landscape. In the distance, I can make out an old farmhouse way up in the hills with two people (probably an elderly husband and his wife - remember Ma and Pa Kettle?) siting on the porch. They were both dressed in overalls, smiling and waving at me while sucking on their corn cob pipes. I was more scared than embarrassed. I was terrified that somehow, I had suddenly entered a 'Twilight Zone' time

warp and become part of the Al Capp comic strip, 'Lil Abner'!!
Only then did it occur to me that I might be arrested by Barney
Fife for indecent exposure and have to spend days behind bars
in their local lock-up. I dashed back to our car while holding up
my pants with one hand looked at my wife, and explained what
had transpired. She just muttered, "I hope you're proud of
yourself!" Then she rolled her eyes - yet again. My daughter
would call this kind of experience 'a caper'. To this day I'm still
deathly afraid of taking a detour!

I still like to carry maps with me when we're traveling. That's
because one time driving back from Florida, we got hopelessly
lost in rural Kentucky at 2 AM. My wife (our technological co-
pilot) was using the GPS on her cell phone simultaneously with
the GPS on the dashboard of the car. The two GPS voices
began to argue with each other, disagreeing on the best route (I
believe one is named 'Siri'). Next, I heard the other voice say
"your destination is on the right". I thought it sounded eerily like
a female version of Rod Serling at the beginning of a 'Twilight
Zone' episode. As I climbed out of my car in pitch black
darkness, serenaded by crickets and cicadas, I found myself on
a dirt road in the middle of nowhere, starring at a cow. Don't ask
how we finally found our hotel. The point is, what do millennials
do when they can't use their GPS or cell phone devises, hope for
the best? Believe you me, they'll wish they had a map!

How did the airlines come up with the concept of 'First Class'? Undoubtedly, it was purely a profit deal – in other words it had nothing to do with the extra attention and preferential treatment afforded those passengers." "Let's see, how can we encourage these idiots to pay more money to buy a ticket on a flight from Detroit to Cleveland?" "I know, the fluffy, unstained pillow and gourmet cookie should do the trick, after all it's only a twenty-five-minute flight." Do 'first class' passengers really feel more important or privileged – they're only separated from the common folk by a thin, dirty, threadbare piece of cloth! I'll bet they would feel safer if there was better security between them and the riffraff. I envision a scene someday where a total revolt takes place at 30,000 feet, and the 'coach class' people rush the 'first class' seating section. "We're mad as Hell, and we're not going to take it anymore!" It would be like witnessing the storming of the Bastille or Santa Anna taking the Alamo. In the old days aboard ocean-going ships, proper class distinction was more clearly, and safely, defined. You were either in 'first class', 'second class', or 'steerage' (the cheapest) and each section occupied a separate deck – steerage being the lowest. Remember the locked iron gates between decks in the movie 'Titanic'? That sure kept 'em in their place, didn't it! By the way, what about the airplane pilots' position in all of this? They couldn't care less, I'm sure – after all, they bask in luxury themselves, waited on hand and foot by the flight attendants. They are protected from attack by a locked iron door with the 'air marshals' close at hand for protection.   It's sort of ironic and archaic that we still allow class distinction of this sort in the 21st century! Just because they have more money, should they enjoy better treatment than the rest of us?   Ah, the stuff that 'class action' law suits are made of and the tabloids feed on!   How come social media hasn't weighed in on this?

Here's a thought; when you start out on a trip and attempt to get driving directions on Map Quest or Google, why don't they skip the first three or four numbered directions and just start with a street name you don't recognize?   Don't they think I can find my way out of my own neighborhood? Before towns and villages began actually coming up with specific street names and permanent signs, residents used natural markers in order to find their way around. If you wanted to travel to another nearby town or strike out to find a new place, you simply took note of prominent objects along the route.   "You make a left at the walnut grove, then right at the big rock that looks like a duck, then straight through the little gulch, then curve left around Miller's pond, then take the next right at the big oak tree, then over the hill with the pine trees on top, then past the old mill, then..." well, you get the idea. It was easy to locate the objects and find your way to and from the next town. It was very easy to give directions to others as well. All you had to do was reverse the route to get home again. To make sure you didn't get lost, they began to draw diagrams and sketches (maps) to show the way. All of this worked quite well until someone moved the rock, cut down the tree, or the old tavern burned down. Eventually, however, this is how street names evolved over the years. Towns had streets named Cherry Lane, Pine Ridge, and, Maple Grove. They also began to name them after prominent citizens. The early method of creating boundaries to establish land ownership, easements, and other rights of way were called 'metes and bounds' descriptions. Sometimes, years later, land surveyors made mistakes and road names became inadvertently misspelled. As an example, we have a local street in our town called 'Old Perch' which was actually originally platted as 'Old Peach'. How someone can confuse a fish with a fruit, I don't know. Getting back to my original thoughts on Map Quest, GPS, and the like, everything today involving this technology is very useful until you don't have a good satellite signal or lose your wireless connection. Then you're really up the proverbial creek without any paddle. Maybe it's time, just as a backup plan mind you, we consider going back to rocks and trees.

Going through security check at the airport is always a treat. The other day, a lady in a wheelchair set off the alarm - imagine that! The 'gendarmes' began to pat her down while waving the electric wand all over her body. C'mon, either they have to use a little common sense or the manufacturers have to start making the chairs entirely out of plastic! The next guy was told to remove his belt before walking through the detector and when he obeyed, his pants fell to the floor. Another example involved body piercings under clothing which set off the machine. Last time I checked, tiny metal body piercings were not weapons. What's next, electric cattle prods? All of us in line behind these poor people felt empathy and embarrassment for them. By the same token, we were wary of saying anything for fear of being hauled off to a work camp or road chain gang and never seen or heard from again. Has it really come to the point of humiliating people in order to protect everyone? Personally, I think some of the TSA agents are on a power trip and need to be a little friendlier toward and more respectful of the passengers coming through the line.

Lately there have been examples of lap top computers catching fire and actually exploding in the cargo area of airplanes. Apparently, there's no need for a terrorist to actually trigger some explosive device, it happens all by itself. Nice to know we've finally found a way to beat the terrorists at their own game! The authorities, however, in their wisdom, have decided this is definitely a hazard and will now only allow them to be carried onboard by passengers (if you have them in an approved 'butterfly' bag). So, it's better that these devices should ignite and then explode right in your face? What about the passenger next to or near you? What about exploding pants, shoes, or socks? Should we all now have the right to bring aboard our own fire extinguisher? I suppose they could ban all types of

82

devices entirely, right? I doubt it. Maybe the pilots could keep them for safe keeping in the cockpit. Maybe the TSA checkers could tag them and hold them for you until your return. That would certainly speed up the lines at security, wouldn't it? It also makes me feel much safer! Hey wait, I know - maybe the laptop manufacturers could offer to fix them at no cost before they go haywire? Brilliant!

I watched a news story today where an individual was 'banned' from the local airport. Apparently, he had completely destroyed the bathroom aboard an airplane and the airline carrier convinced the airport personnel to forbid him from setting foot in their facility again. This reminds me of the old 'Seinfeld' episode where Kramer is banned from shopping at the local fruit market. He desires the especially good tasting fruit so much that he enlists the help of Jerry and Newman as stand-ins to shop for him. As usual, it doesn't turn out very well for Kramer – but it's funny. If, in fact, this bathroom man is clearly to blame for the restroom mischief and is known to the authorities, how about just arresting the felon instead? If allowed to go 'free', what other crimes will he commit? What I don't get is how are they realistically going to prevent him from getting into the airport? Are they going to distribute post office type mug shots of the culprit all over the airport terminal? Will the airport post armed guards all around, resembling a third world country? What if he's a master of disguise and can elude the TSA staff? If a passenger actually recognizes the man, what is he/she supposed to do about it? "I think I just saw that guy who trashed the bathroom on the airplane, somebody stop him!!

While driving my car the other day, a notice appeared on the dashboard screen. It warned about the danger of taking your eyes off of the road while driving. Why would they actually tempt you to take your eyes off the road to read a message about not taking your eyes off the road? I just don't get it! Another time, I received a message about being more careful when driving after dark. Don't they actually mean AFTER LIGHT?

Apparently, there are new state laws being enacted across the country affecting the use of cell phones while crossing the street. You may still legally talk on your phone while walking through an intersection, however, you will be fined if you are caught looking down at your phone while crossing. Has common sense left us completely? Is this behavior yet another example of our 'me first', first amendment rights mentality? We now have to spend millions to try to protect these idiots from themselves! If they were injured would their first reaction be to sue the car owner? I'm sorry, but I just don't get it. So, it's still alright to look at your phone while driving, but not while walking? So, I should kill someone with my car rather than be killed by a car as a pedestrian?

When new streets are created or resurfaced, why do the engineers insist upon locating the sewer covers right where your tires are going to run over them? Couldn't they be placed in the middle of the road or off to the far-right hand side near the curb so you don't drive over them constantly? Most roads are elevated in the center and drain toward the edge anyway. If you have an older, classic or antique vehicle, you avoid running over them like the plague because the jolt is so severe that you risk losing parts of your car when you hit them. They're as bad as some of our worst potholes. It's like driving across an old railroad track. Shrapnel actually flies off the car and you can lose fillings in your teeth to boot! I know it's a little thing, and I should be thankful that they are making an effort to resurface and improve our roads and bridges, but for heaven's sake, use your head! Speaking of driving through road construction areas, why do you never actually see anyone working? All of the orange barrels are in place, and the blockade signs are up (sometimes for months), but I've rarely seen anyone present at all. Are they invisible or do they only quietly show up to work between midnight and 6am? Some of the most nerve racking, on-going road work has existed for years along I-75 between Cincinnati and Dayton, Ohio. I think it's become a permanent deal. I wouldn't be surprised if it's soon designated as a national historic site!

When you drive out of our Florida condo complex, you immediately encounter a divided highway with a large grassy boulevard separating east from west bound traffic. It presents a very dangerous situation for any driver, let alone senior citizens. There's an opening in the median directly across from you which allows you to go straight through or turn left. Traffic from both directions can also use this as a way to make a 'u turn'. Drivers could actually be attempting fourteen different maneuvers at this one small intersection simultaneously! You could get killed 'eight ways to Sunday', as the old expression goes. Suffice it to say, this is an accident just waiting to happen. In fact, there have been several fender benders over the years as well as two fatal accidents at the location. The local city town council has been approached more than once to have a safety traffic signal installed, but has taken no action as yet. One council member went on record saying they are waiting for a third fatal crash to occur before they make any safety changes. Are they nuts? Should we solicit volunteers?

"To market, to market" ...

Recently, I found myself in a fresh food market that offered both free samples and bulk food – right next to each other. Pretty hard to distinguish between the two if you ask me. I fancied some roasted peanuts so I pulled down the lever and 3 came out (actually, 3 half peanuts to be exact). The manager came running over and accused me of stealing. Shocked, I held out my hand so he could see the 3 half peanuts and exclaimed I was only trying a 'free sample'. How are you supposed to know if it's 'free' or not? How do you know if you want to buy some if you don't taste it first, right? I pointed out a lady down the aisle sampling grapes out of the bag at the fruit stand, and he became even more enraged. The veins were bulging on his forehead. I thought sirens, bells, whirling lights, and whistles were going to go off and he was going to call the police! Instead, he told me to leave the store – fine way to treat a good customer! I suppose I could have done what Uncle Leo did on the Seinfeld episode where he's accused of shop-lifting in a bookstore. I could have said (in a loud voice for all to hear) "I'm an old man, I forgot!" before they arrested me and hauled me off to the slammer. I don't think he used good judgement, then again, apparently neither did I!

I recently bought some very good (and extremely expensive) chocolate at a Canadian retail candy shop. The employees were very friendly and helpful. The store offered quite an assortment of candy, but no prices were shown. On the counter, next to the cash register, which they call a 'till', stood a very large sign which read:

This Register Only Accepts:

Visa

MasterCard

Debit

NO CASH

(Sorry for the inconvenience)

If they really wanted to get their point across and avoid subsequent embarrassment at the 'till', why didn't they post their sign on the outside of the entrance door? Probably not a good idea either. God forbid they should discourage any customers from actually coming into the store. Once inside, customers would probably pay 'an arm and a leg' for the rather pricey chocolate (which is exactly what I did). The owner knows you will be hooked by the sights and smells and unable to leave without buying something (unless you only had cash on you). You can bet they don't call the only 'till' in their store a 'cash register' – because they won't accept cash!   Don't the employees know how to make change? Isn't the owner paying an extra fee every time he accepts payment by credit card? Our relatives would be rolling over in their graves if they found out "We don't accept cash anymore"!

About ten or twelve years ago, 'dollar stores' began to pop up around the country - undoubtedly in response to the national economic downturn. I thought they would be a 'flash in the pan', however, they're still around today.   Most of the items found there are, in fact, priced at $1.00. At first, I sort of felt sorry for the shoppers who frequented these stores - thinking they were disadvantaged and couldn't afford to spend a lot of money. These low-priced stores truly offered a real benefit for the less privileged.   For some strange reason, I even felt sad for the employees who worked there. Then I started to see rich people pull into the parking lots in their Audi's, BMW's, and Cadillacs. Is this how they got to be rich?   Did they know something that I didn't? Should they even be allowed to shop there? They have a lot of nerve (and apparently no shame) running through the store gobbling up every low-priced item off the shelf.   Soon they'll be demanding a 'clearance' section in the store with items reduced to fifty cents. They're gonna ruin a good thing. The end result of this will surely be higher prices.   Soon these 'dollar stores' will be replaced by the 'two-dollar stores'.   I hope they don't go the way of the 'five & ten' and Woolworths!

Who thought up the name for the store 'Bed, Bath, and, Beyond?' It begs the questions, 'Beyond what'? or 'What's Beyond Bed and Bath? Is the correct answer 'a shower'? Or, 'a nap'? Or, 'your wildest imagination'? Or 'Death'? I think once they created the store, they offered so many different kinds of stuff, they couldn't fit it all in the name. It would cost a small fortune to make up signs that huge – and they would weigh a ton. Boy, if you can't find what you're looking for in one of their stores, you ain't gonna find it anywhere!

I went into the neighborhood CVS and decided to buy a few bars of soap. All the packages I looked at were called 'moisturizer bars' or 'beauty bars'. Not one label used the word 'soap' anywhere on the package! Being confused (and not wanting to buy the wrong stuff), I went to the cashier and asked her where they stocked the bar soap. She pointed me toward the aisle marked 'body care'. Now, to be completely honest, most of this merchandise is clearly meant for women. You would think that would make it easier for men to find what they want. Not so. I personally believe that's because there's way too much choice available. Anyway, the bar soap situation was quickly resolved by my wife as she dropped a package in our cart. I asked her how she knew it was soap and she said, "Never mind, it's what you always use." At the same time, she automatically determined she had a coupon for half off that brand of soap. Nicely done!

We have four or five upscale fruit and vegetable stores in our area that compete with each other for business. I think most shoppers would consider them 'gourmet', ethnic type markets, displaying freshness and quality. They seem to do a brisk business – the aisles are always crowded. They stand in contrast to the large chain grocery stores like Kroger, Publix, and Winn-Dixie. In one such store there is a paper notice pasted on the glass case containing delicious pastries and cakes which reads, 'Keep Moving!' I didn't get it at first. Why would they discourage everyone from stopping to look at, and hopefully purchase, deserts in the case? Upon closer inspection, there is a tiny mitten shown between the words Keep and Moving, which is a symbol for the state of Michigan. It's sends a completely different message. They want you to be aware the items are home grown in Michigan. There must be a future to these 'fresh market' stores. Amazon certainly thinks so because they bought and invested a lot of money in Whole Foods. These newer gourmet fruit and vegetable markets are probably another throw-back to the days of the beloved 'mom and pop' markets of our youth. They sure had a feel good, inviting, friendly atmosphere, and everything smelled great!

The guy who came up with the idea for manufacturing and selling bottled water must be worth a gazillion dollars. What I don't get is why buy it bottled when you can get it right out of your kitchen faucet (which you've already paid for anyway)? I know, I know, people say it's much safer to drink and it's portable (not to be confused with potable water). All you need to do is get an insulated thermos and keep refilling it. When we were kids, in the summertime, we used to take a drink right from the garden hose and never got sick. In the winter, we would break off icicles and eat them as well. In fact, you're probably drinking tap water when you put ice cubes in your drink. I think the guy who thought up the bottled water deal was formerly a doctor who kept harping on the importance of staying hydrated. Doctors still recommend drinking eight glasses of water each day to avoid dehydration. I think I'll probably get thirsty before that happens. If there was a broken water main, you just boiled your water for a day or two until they fixed the line. Personally, I don't enjoy drinking plain water due to the fact that fish swim in it! Then there's the concept of Starbucks coffee. Thirty-some years ago, a friend of mine in Ohio called and told me about a new company that was going public. He was thinking about buying stock and wanted my opinion. He described what the franchise coffee shop would look like and said they felt there was a huge market offering a cup of coffee to customers and charging $5 or so per cup. I actually laughed out loud at the thought of paying that sum when I could make it myself for a lot less. Well, once again the joke was on me. Starbucks is a successful institution today – who would have thought! It proves people really are willing to pay more for quality and convenience.

Speaking of grocery stores and markets, why are there aisles of non-refrigerated packaged meat that reassuringly read "FULLY COOKED"? Would I want to eat it right off the shelf if it said "PARTIALLY OR UNCOOKED"? Of course, it should be obvious (and go without saying) that I would prefer 'FULLY COOKED'. In like fashion, I used to feel comfortable with the phrase 'processed meat' – sounded much safer than eating 'unprocessed meat'. Now the expert health officials recommend completely avoiding 'processed meat' - apparently not healthy for you to consume. Like you're going to drop dead the minute it hits your blood stream! Now we should only eat '100% Pure, organic (and boring/tasteless/bland) Meat'? A well-known bratwurst sausage company has created new products that contain less fat, no added MSG, etc. Their healthier apple chicken sausage is made with 100% 'pure' chicken – it says so in large print right on the package, yet the list of ingredients simply leads off with 'chicken'. I would hope its 'pure' chicken – would you want to eat contaminated or impure chicken? A sign in an upscale grocery market reads, 'local pasture raised chicken and eggs – no antibiotics, no hormones, no GMO's – beyond organic'. What does 'beyond organic' mean? Another one reads, 'humanely raised – 100% vegetarian feed'. Does this mean we're going to discard and not eat them if they were raised 'inhumanely'? Are we supposed to feel sorry for them if they were underprivileged or came from a poor or abusive home environment? Did these animals decide for themselves to switch to a vegan life style?

Staying on the topic of grocery stores, I get confused when they advertise 'buy one, get one free' on some items and then in the next isle a different item has a sign that says '2 for $10'. Obviously, they don't mean the same thing, right? The issue for me (because I have nothing else to think about, I guess) is what price do I pay if I only want one, not two of these things? I can assure you the employees don't know either. If you stop one to ask them how much one costs, they have to ask their manager or call the home office in Bismarck, North Dakota to find out! It really doesn't matter because two minutes after they give me the answer, I've forgotten anyway. Apparently, one means you pay full price for one and the other means you pay half the price of two. For me, it's like trying to remember the difference between a tablespoon and a teaspoon – very confusing!

Another thing I simply don't get involves store sales and coupons. I realize it's a ploy to attract customers, however, wouldn't it be easier to just advertise everyday low prices instead? Most of the area store sales state 'limited time offer', or 'sale ends Friday', and my luck is to always find out about the sale on the very last day. The crazy thing is that typically a new sale starts right after the previous one ends, and new coupons are printed every week. Do they take us for idiots? I should probably claim the 5th on that.

Why is it that many people will wear anything and everything to Publix markets and Walmart? Are they not embarrassed – have they no shame? Some of these stores still have scales to weigh yourself when you enter. While they're at it, how about mirrors? Are they so desperate for business that they'll let everyone in who's not naked? Some stores and restaurants still require shirts and shoes be worn in order to receive service – 'Proper Dress Required'. I guess everyone's definition of 'proper' is different, isn't it?

Is there a doctor in the house? ...

Recently I received a Medicare health assessment questionnaire in the mail. Question 18 reads (and I'm not making this up), 'Did you fall during the last 12 months'? Then it actually defines the term 'fall': 'A fall is when your body goes to the ground without being pushed.' Seriously? Really? What imbecile doesn't understand what it means to fall down? I recall the Groucho Marx line, "I may sound like an idiot, and look like an idiot, but make no mistake, I really am an idiot"! In reality, falls are apparently the second-leading cause of death by injury, right behind car accidents. This is especially true if you happen to fall from Niagara Falls. Remember the joke, "It's not the fall that hurts, it's hitting the ground!" I'll bet the same people who worked on this Medicare questionnaire produced the medical alert device TV commercial, "I've fallen and I can't get up". It's like when you're in the hospital and all the nurses feel they have to talk to you in a very loud voice. They must think everyone our age is deaf. Either that or we've forgotten how to respond to English. Either way, it's frustrating, but sometimes comical.

Another thing I find annoying today are automated phone message systems. When you call your doctor's office (or any company for that matter) you don't get a live person, instead you are greeted by a pre-recorded message or voice mail.   I understand this is much more economical – it's too expensive, after all, for them to actually employ a real person. In reality, It's a profit deal. So you are given a series of options: "Press 1 if you know your parties extension", "Press 2 if you don't know your parties extension", "Press 3 to get directions to our office", "Press 4 if you no longer own a vehicle or your license has been revoked", Press 5 if you don't have an electric lift chair and need help getting up", "Press 6 if you're calling from a memory care facility or maximum security prison", "Press 7 if you're still there and are feeling nauseated, or can't hear me anymore", or… "Press 99 if you would like to return to the main menu". (YIKES!! Anything but THAT!) By the time you've reached the end of your options, you've either slipped into a coma, passed away, or at the very least forgotten why you called in the first place. Sometimes, the reason you called doesn't have an option assigned to it – then what are you supposed to do? To be really fair, I think the tables should be turned. The president or CEO should have to call in every morning and be forced to go through the complete list of options themselves on a daily basis.   They deserve to be nauseated along with us!   Telemarketers are getting pretty sneaky lately as well. They've started calling using a local area code rather than a toll-free exchange so you think it might be someone you know. If I recognize the number because they have called before, I answer using an English accent or reply in German, just to get their reaction and test their patience.

98

Pretending to be hard of hearing drives 'em nuts too. I'm even tempted to tell them to wait a minute while I check with my wife and then put them on hold for an hour.

Pharmaceutical companies that manufacture and sell prescription drugs are required to list the possible adverse effects or 'side effects', as they're called, on the bottles and in their television commercials. Thousands of clinical trials are undertaken to record all of the reactions to ingesting various drugs prior to approval by our FDA. My question is, unless you are desperately ill and willing to risk anything to feel better, who do they get to take part in these experiments? Are death row prison inmates, illegal aliens, or income tax evaders subjected to secret testing of every new drug before it appears on the market? Some of these side effects are relatively minor while others are serious and down-right scary! Under the heading of minor adverse annoyances, you would probably find: skin rash, itching, drowsiness, wheezing, diarrhea, joint pain, headache, stomach pain, belching, constipation, heartburn, nausea, sweating, trouble sleeping, vomiting, blurred vision, etc. The category of serious would include: internal bleeding, trouble breathing, irregular heartbeat, thoughts of suicide, inflammation of your pancreas, low blood sugar, kidney problems, swelling of your face, lips, tongue or throat, fainting, gallbladder problems, hallucinations, coma, muscle twitching, high or low blood pressure, fever, changes in vision, reckless behavior, talking more or faster than usual, excessive happiness or irritability, actually never getting to sleep or waking up again, the urge to run out and get a gun permit, looking forward to going shopping at the mall on black Friday, or (the big one) DEATH itself! Now tell me this, you know the part where it says, "Avoid taking this medication, or tell your doctor, if you experience any of these symptoms?" How on earth can you tell your doctor anything if you are DEAD! Do these risks really out-way the benefits of the drug? How long do you have to wait to find out if you're dead?

Why do doctors and hospitals continue to charge you more for services and tests than the insurance industry will normally accept? Surely, they have access to information about reasonable reimbursement costs and know ahead of time how much they should be charging. I think what they're banking on is you haven't as yet met your co-pay or annual deductible and you will have to pay the difference. If you don't even have the most 'affordable insurance coverage' you will more than likely get stuck with the entire overinflated bill. Medical insurance is certainly necessary for major illness expense, however, if you are reasonably healthy and don't visit the doctor often, it can seem like you're not getting your money's worth. From a dollars and cents standpoint, if you don't use it enough to meet your annual deductible or co-pay limits (which can be a lot), you are paying premiums without much benefit. Why don't they give you a break if you don't have many medical claims and you're not going to cost them much money? Like full coverage (without premiums, co-pays or deductibles) for the following year! Now there's a real incentive to be proactive and try to stay healthy! Sounds fair to me! How come our congressional representatives (i.e. politicians) can't work with our insurance carriers and come up with some plan like this? They probably don't really care much because they don't have to worry about paying for their insurance.

A local hospital prominently displays a sign in the lobby area which proudly reads, 'A Top 10 Hospital in our Metropolitan Area'. I didn't even realize there were that many local hospitals in our area. I'd be hard pressed to name more than four or five! Does this claim make sense to anyone? Should they really be boasting about this accomplishment? When you really examine the numbers, what does it mean? What survey criteria are used in the ranking process? On the one hand, if there are 100, you can probably feel safe in going there. If, on the other hand, there are exactly ten, where does this one rank? If this facility is number nine or (Lord forbid!) ten, what does that tell you? You probably wouldn't want to be caught dead there, even though they would make every effort to save your life! Just make sure you have your DNR paperwork on file!

Going to the dentist can be a trip. As a matter of fact, when we were kids, our dentist was actually named 'Doctor Tripp'. For real. My two brothers and I would sit in the small lobby awaiting our turn to see Dr. Tripp and his torture chamber room. I think my Dad would have felt better about his kids having to go to the dentist if they could have anesthetized his wallet! That's not really fair, as Dr. Tripp was actually a very nice man. All those strange looking sharp metal instruments resting on the shiny tray were, however, pretty scary and intimidating! We would flip a coin to determine which of us would go first. My younger brother didn't really care because he never had any cavities anyway – he never got the Novocain shot, felt the nerve pain of the drill, or smelled his tooth burning red-hot. It wasn't because he brushed and flossed regularly (which he didn't), he simply had a hard enamel coating on his teeth which was impervious to decay. It resembled armor plating but was rather greenish yellow in color. We referred to him as 'ole moss-back'. He had no problem actually volunteering to go first. He would later return to the waiting area grinning in victory. My youngest brother and I weren't as fortunate. We, apparently, had soft tooth enamel with the consistency of marshmallow. We definitely felt and smelled the dreaded drill each and every visit. Dr. Tripp always had magazines in his lobby featuring the latest in grotesque dental reconstructive surgery – it was one of those deals (like a car accident or train wreck) where you couldn't look away. They were horrifying! The stuff nightmares were made of. Why on earth did he leave them lying around in plain sight of impressionable young kids? Maybe he was psychotic. Did he think seeing those poor deformed faces would soften your fear and anxiety? Like, nothing he's gonna do to me could possibly be that bad!

One thing we all have in common during our visits to the dentist is trying to talk clearly with cotton baton stuffed around our gums or a clay-like mold stuck to our teeth for an impression. Why does the dentist or his dental assistant insist on asking us questions (or making small talk) when they know our response will most certainly be unintelligible? Question: "So, what grade are you in now?" Answer: "umph, kwaide". Are they sadistic or just have a rather warped sense of humor? I was always temped to respond in German just to see if he was paying attention. For that matter, I suppose I could have attempted sign language, had I taken the time to learn it. Scenes from 'Marathon Man' with poor Dustin Hoffman wriggling in the chair raced in my brain. My wife and her siblings went to a dentist who actually smoked cigarettes while working on their teeth! The smell coming off of those yellow stained fingers literally made them gag. She claims her first root canal was without the benefit of Novocain. Dr. Dementia (not his real name) told her the root was dead and she probably wouldn't feel any pain – easy for him to say (as the tears rolled down her cheeks). Unbelievable! Remember those plastic fake teeth wind-up toys when we were kids? Chattering choppers – hilarious gag! If I ever reach the point where I have to wear actual false teeth (fake choppers), I think I'll try throwing them in the dishwasher to clean them rather than paying to have the hygienist do it!

In a recent issue of Reader's Digest, a segment labeled 'News from the World of Medicine' revealed that skin cancers may reduce the risk of getting Alzheimer's disease. Kinda makes you want to run out to the tanning booth, doesn't it? So, does this infer overexposure to the sun (as well as a lifetime of trips to the dermatologist) will result in you not losing your mind? Will you die from melanoma cancer before you lose your marbles? Pick your poison. Another study in the same article claims just ten minutes of exercise each day will improve memory. So, if you forget to exercise one morning, you run the risk of getting permanent amnesia? Sounds more like an ad from a local gym. Yet another section offers, 'if people take at least five really hot baths every week, they would have significantly lower markers for atherosclerosis.' So, if you purposely scald yourself, or risk ending up resembling a prune for life, you will at least be 'heart healthy'? Should we consider extending the length of time we spend in a hot tub? Here's the last RD article that struck me as pretty bizarre. This one is labeled 'Poor Hearing Doubles Injury Risk". A survey of seven million people (which is a lot, right?) revealed that "those who experienced a lot of trouble hearing were roughly twice as likely to get hurt in an accident." Seriously? You mean to tell me that people who are hard of hearing may get injured more often than people who don't have impaired hearing? Isn't this rather like stating the obvious? Bystander- "Hey, look out buddy, there's a truck coming right at you!!" Second bystander - "Oh, don't even bother trying to warn him, he can't hear you anyway!" Did any of these studies actually make the American Medical Journal?

'It's none of your business' ...

I went to my bank the other day to deposit a check. When the transaction was finished, I asked if I might use their bathroom. The assistant manager looked at me like I was nuts and stated they had no public restrooms. Employees only. I tactfully reminded him that even CVS, Jo-Ann Fabrics, and every grocery store I could think of gladly let their customers use the restroom. Besides, I was their customer, had just deposited more money with them, and, had several accounts there. Did I really have to say this? I stopped short of telling him to look at the tape on his camera. He then went to his manager to ask for an exception to this rule. Seriously! I felt like I just got approved for a loan when he said they would make an exception in my case. By this time, I had to go so bad my legs were crossed standing in the lobby. How many other 'customers' have had to go through this embarrassment? The thing I really don't get is they had four keypad bathrooms and four employees – talk about private banking!

Fabric stores have a department called 'Notions'. Saleslady: "May I help you"? Me: "Yes, I'm looking for a (fill in the blank)". Saleslady: "Oh, that would be in 'NOTIONS". What the heck are 'Notions'? I have a good notion to ask the manager what a notion is!   Similarly, where did the word 'hardware store' originate?   This is not to be confused with today's computer 'software'.

Our most popular local law firms repeatedly advertise on TV that they are always 'fighting' for you in court.   This is undoubtedly to assure you that they are working as hard as they can, and spending big bucks, to get you off the hook, or win the best settlement. If in fact, they were actually constantly fighting in the courtroom, wouldn't the bailiffs break it up and arrest them? Then they'd be hunting down a barrister to come to their rescue. Now that would truly be 'Breaking News'!

So, they name many of the rental car companies 'Budget', 'Dollar', 'Thrifty', etc. If people rent cars from them, why do they complain if something goes wrong with the car? They sought out the lowest cost deal, right?   What do they expect?   The old phrase, "you get what you pay for" comes to mind here.   When you go for cheap, sometimes you get cheap!

Why are there so many antique shops and dealers around today? What's the appeal of so much old stuff (junk) and how do these people make a living? Who actually purchases this bric-a-brac anyway? If you do buy something in one of these stores, it usually ends up going to a subdivision garage sale someday. My wife and I were recently in a tiny town in Canada which sported 5 antique shops – I'm not even sure the little village had a post office. It is said, 'One man's junk is another man's treasure', right?   When you consider all of the ongoing garage sales, rummage sales, consignment shops, and the like, antique shops have a lot of competition (and a lot of dust!). I think I developed allergies by just walking through one. The people who own and operate these shops must be very 'thick-skinned' because they take a lot of rejection from a lot of 'tire-kickers'.   It probably comes down to sentimentality and nostalgia – "My mother had one just like that". It undoubtedly reflects a longing for the past (the good old days of our youth) which, sadly, can never return.

I was always fascinated by watching and listening to a ventriloquist. In reality, everyone probably really focuses on the 'dummy', not the ventriloquist. Why do they call him a 'dummy' anyway? He's the one finishing all the punch lines and getting all the laughs, so he's really the smart one!   Fred Russell is widely regarded as the father of modern ventriloquism, based in London, England.   There have been many very talented ventriloquists over the years – Edgar Bergen, Señor Wences, Jimmy Nelson, Shari Lewis, just to name a few. By far and away, my favorite was Paul Winchell.   His puppets Jerry Mahoney and Knucklehead Smiff were legendary and the dialogue was hysterical while often endearing.   I'm told the Smithsonian in Washington DC holds the originals in storage. Although he led a very sad life, suffering from child abuse, depression and multiple troubled marriages, Winch, as he was affectionately known, was quite an avid inventor. Among many patented inventions, he is credited with designing the first artificial heart along with Dr. Henry Heimlich (who also invented the Heimlich maneuver). Ventriloquism was developed by the early Greeks and had its origins in religious belief. Later, they became part of the performing arts genre, gaining popularity in England's music halls, and vaudeville in America. The ability to 'throw' one's voice is pretty amazing. Some can even project their voice to the puppet dummy while drinking a glass of water! How do they do that? They can also pronounce difficult consonants with their lips parted, using combinations of sounds to sound to the listener like b, d, v, etc. Part of the interest is watching an inanimate object be made to 'come to life' and carry on a lively and funny conversation. The 'act' often involved the dummy getting the best of the puppeteer. It's a real talent – very creative stuff!

'Death, be not proud'...

W hy do older people feel they have to 'one up you' or 'top you' when you engage in a conversation about medical ailments? Is it a game of 'I'm sicker than you' or 'have pity on me because I am worse off', or 'I always have bad luck and I'm really sick all the time'? Are they close to knocking on 'Death's Door"? Or maybe it's just that they want to finally win at something before they die or simply forget what's happened to them. It's like dueling banjos. You can tell they're not even listening to you, they're already anxious to tell you about the botched surgery or near-death experiences they've had. Around the pool in Florida, I've devised a list of our most commonly or frequently discussed topics. We actually often test it out with new acquaintances as well (while smiling knowingly and reassuringly at each other in the process). Among the topics are restaurants (some we've tried and liked, some we've never tried but heard good things about, some that are way too expensive, some where we've experienced terrible service, and, those to stay away from at all costs). Speaking of Florida restaurants, I've always wondered why these snowbirds arrive and end up having dinner with friends and relatives from back home. Do they miss them that much? Have they no other friends? Shouldn't they try to make new friends? Many rarely get together with most of these people while at home anyway! Other frequent conversation topics include the weather back home, the grandkids, as well as how long it took them to get to Florida. Topping the list by far, without question, is the dialogue about medical ailments.   One of my friends started coughing and said he thought he accidentally swallowed a 'no see um' bug. I said, how can you tell? You can't see um! For that matter, how can you avoid or kill um if you can't see um?

There seems to be an explosion of very expensive independent, assisted living and memory care facilities being built today in our area. I understand the rationale behind this proliferation of senior citizen housing construction, what with the millions of 'baby boomers' entering their golden years. What I question is, are there really that many of us who can afford to lay out $6,000 to 10,000 per month to live in one of these developments? I doubt the owners are willing to accept payment from Medicare or Medicaid and they probably won't be subsidized from other sources either.   Are there enough rich people to fill them up?   Do these wealthy people in effect overpay themselves and thereby somehow help out those unable to pay? They better be building a lot more less costly, yet acceptable, places to accommodate the millions who can't afford this expensive level of care. If there aren't enough alternatives available, what are people going to do? Where are they going to put them?   The days of seniors living with their children are fading away. What if you sign up for a ritzy place and after a few months can no longer afford to live there, do they put you and your stuff out on the curb? I'm fearful that many of us may be in for a very rude awakening. I remember the movie 'Soylent Green', do you?

I received a flyer in the mail while in Florida this past Winter. It advertised a free lunch and informational seminar on the benefits of preplanning your cremation. Perfect, I thought! I can get a free lunch, make final plans involving what to do with myself post death, and assuredly get more fodder for this book - all at the same time, in one afternoon. Deals like this don't come along every week - usually it's every other week. The flyer went on to offer a chance to win a raffle for a free seven-day cruise for two. Now I'm thinking, "What if I win the cruise, but I've already been cremated?" It doesn't say, 'must be present to win'. Does my wife still get to go and bring me along in an urn? Maybe she could toss my ashes over the side of the boat or spread them on a beach in Hawaii! Either way, this whole deal sounded too good to pass up. Two seminar dates were offered, both a day of two before Valentine's Day. Great timing, I thought. If I played my cards right, this could also count as going out to celebrate Valentine's Day! This event was sponsored by the National Cremation Society, not to be confused with the Dead Poets Society. The fine print indicated the offer was void in several states in the US, Guam, Puerto Rico, the Virgin Islands, and where prohibited by law. It also clearly stated, 'only for first time adult attendees interested in cremation'. Why would you go if you weren't interested - twice? What are they serving for lunch, anyway? Why has this ploy been prohibited in certain areas? Do they know something we don't? Nevertheless, I was getting excited even though I had lots of serious questions before I summoned up the courage to reserve a spot. After all my planning, my wife put the kibosh on going by reminding me we had already purchased cemetery burial plots!

On a somewhat related topic, I was taking my morning walk around the development and noticed a restoration company truck parked outside a condo near our unit. The name written on side of the truck was (and I'm not making this up) 'I am Mold'. Obviously, they deal with restoration from water and mold damage, probably from failed air conditioning systems. I'll bet no one realized the play on words 'I am old' – very fitting for a company working predominantly with senior citizens.

I finally discontinued my subscription to the daily local newspaper. I found, even as a retiree, that I didn't really have the time to read the entire paper – they started to pile up. I would read the sections which held the most interest for me – sports and business. I also began to glance at the obituaries section. Then I started to actually scour it, looking for the names of people I knew - a truly scary proposition. George Burns, the famous comic, said he used to wake up each morning, read the obits, and if he didn't see his name listed, he would get out of bed and start his day. What is this curiosity we have with death? It's part of life, right? I think it's the finality of it and the uncertainty of what happens next. The great magician and escape artist Harry Houdini vowed to his wife that he would come back or at least make contact with her after he died – she never heard from him again after he passed away. As far as I know, no one has every returned in any shape or form, contrary to what the horror movies would have you believe. Death is not only an accepted fact of life, but is often celebrated throughout the world. Mexico and Central America honor their dead with a holiday, the Day of the Dead. The ancient Egyptians were probably the most famous for their fascination by mummifying their deceased pharaohs and building exquisite tombs containing everything needed for the afterlife. Osiris was their god or king of the dead. Unique to western culture is the practice of holding séances to attempt to contact the dead through use of a psychic medium. Even Walt Disney's exposure to and curiosity about death as a child was reflected in some of his full-length feature animated films. Some individuals are so obsessed with the morbidity of death, they get caught up in the phenomenon known as 'Dark Tourism'. As explained in an article (March 2007) in 'New Scientist', if you've been to world war battlefields in northern France, the site of the 9/11 terrorist attacks in New York, a Holocaust museum or even a military cemetery, then you've

115

unknowingly been part of Dark Tourism. Apparently, it's become popular now to visit places where some have died in tragic or spectacular ways – more than half a million people visit the extermination camps of Auschwitz-Birkenau each year. It's not really a new phenomenon, however – just a new label. Tourists have been visiting graves of martyrs for ages and public executions were once a popular spectacle both here and in Europe. People do it for a number of reasons. Normal people are scared of the unknown and death is one of the biggest unknowns. I think the bottom line is as long as you don't get a death wish yourself, but are just curious, I guess it's fine. Comedian Jerry Seinfeld is quoted as saying, "The greatest fear humans have is public speaking – the second greatest fear is death. So, if you happen to be attending a funeral service, you'd rather be in the casket than delivering the eulogy." Funny analogy! This reminds me of the story about the undertaker who spoke with the elderly widow just before the funeral service for her late husband was to begin. He asked her how old her husband was. The widow replied, "97, a year older than me". Then she whispered to him, "It hardly seems worthwhile to go back home, does it?" The big question I have is when a person dies in his sleep, is it true he doesn't know about it until the next morning? I could wake up one morning and find out I'm gone!

I loved the field of archeology as a kid – reading about the discovery of King Tut's tomb was fascinating and exciting stuff. I probably liked the concept as a possible career because you could play in the dirt all day and maybe, if you were lucky, even find something dead. I never really worried about curses for disturbing the dead either. I figured I had bigger things to deal with. Now that I'm an older grown up, I'm also a big fan of genealogical research, but I'm totally not sure why it holds such fascination and interest for me. My young granddaughter sees me discovering and adding more and more ancestors to my family tree and says, "Grandpa's playing among the dead people again". Maybe it's because I'm reassured that they're actually deceased and I'm not - at least I still feel alive, sometimes. In the Netflix movie, "The Last Laugh", one character said we're not old, just 'pre-dead'. There's a very funny scene in the Monty Python movie, "The Holy Grail", where, during the bubonic plague, a wooden cart is being driven down the muddy streets in an English village collecting corpses. The driver repeatedly calls out, "Bring out ya dead", as fake bodies (very realistic looking dummies) are tossed up onto the ever-growing pile on the cart. As the next victim is about to be thrown onto the cart he says, "Wait, I'm not dead yet"! Guess it was hard to tell the difference - but that's how I feel when I'm working on my family tree.

As we get older, do we really resemble or actually become like our fathers or mothers? I've heard people say, "He looks just like his father, or he's acting or saying things just like his father did". I hope we don't turn into our folks because many of them are already dead! Speaking of 'dead', how many times have you heard well-meaning funeral home visitors say "Doesn't he/she look good"? Compared to whom? I know they're trying to be comforting, but come on folks, that person is deceased. I once witnessed a woman leaning over the casket actually talking to the occupant. I heard her say, "By the way Delores, they did a nice job, you look really good!" I strained to hear if the deceased replied, but, of course, heard nothing. It was definitely one of those 'one way' conversations. I wondered if anyone else thought that lady was off her rocker. I also wondered if a ventriloquist had ever been tempted to try out his act in a funeral home. I'm certain that would be frowned upon and strongly discouraged - something about bad taste and the like. Think about it though. If the ventriloquist was also a voice impersonator - now you've really got something! Problem is, you're working a very 'tough crowd'!

Our town council recently approved the construction of a large condominium development. It will consist of six, five-story buildings and an extended boardwalk providing a view of the local river trail below. They are calling this project the Overlook. Are they serious? Didn't anyone involved read the Stephen King novel, "The Shining"? Apparently, the place will cater to 'mature' residents, and the price tags will be between $500,000 and $1 million per unit. Wait 'til they find out it's haunted, start hallucinating, and fall into a time warp as soon as they move in!

It would be like the 'Hotel California' – where you can check-out, but you can never leave! Even better, I'm waiting for some developer to start a new housing subdivision not realizing the land underneath was once a long-forgotten burial ground – think "Poltergeist"! Something to do with life imitating art, I reckon.

I recently celebrated my 70th birthday. Due to a previous heart attack and other medical health issues over the years, I wasn't sure I would live to see the day. Thank God for His mercy. When I turned 50 and even 60, I didn't really think too much about the aging process. Now, at 70, reality is setting in. As they say, 'I'm rounding third base – home plate is in sight'. Other expressions come to mind as well (these are the kind ones):

"You light your birthday cake and a group of campers show up with a bag of marshmallows"

"You drink prune juice…on purpose"

"When you sit down to breakfast, you hear 'snap, crackle, pop…and you haven't even poured your milk yet"

"You play BINGO … and you actually enjoy it"

"Your pharmacist knows you by your first name"

"Your car battery goes dead because your turn signal has been on for two weeks straight"

"You realize that life is like a roll of toilet paper, the closer you get to the end, the faster it goes"

"Your back goes out more often than you do"

When someone says "Nice to see you", you say, "Thanks, I'd rather be seen than viewed"

"Your life insurance company sends you their free annual calendar – one month at a time"

You call the incontinence hotline and they ask, "Can you hold, please?"

"Your body starts making the same noises as your coffee maker"

Why does time seem to go by faster and faster the older you get? Maybe it's because we start to realize we're getting on in life and have less time left. So much to do – so little time! Do everyone's grandchildren grow up as fast as mine? We have ways of measuring and keeping track of it, but we can't see or touch it – sort of the same as seeing the clouds in the sky but not the wind that moves them along. If we don't keep track of it, does it even really exist? Albert Einstein believed time was just an illusion. Does time lapse photography prove time exists? I think everyone would agree that time is fleeting – that it's a way of telling us what's really important. Will Rogers said, "Half our time is spent trying to find something to do with the time we have rushed through life trying to save". Michael Althsuler said, "The bad news is time flies, the good news is you are the pilot". It is also said, 'good things come to those that wait' – so who has the time to wait? How about, 'good things take time' – the truth probably is everything takes up or uses up the precious commodity of time. To paraphrase comic George Carlin, the shortest interval of time is the nano-second between the traffic light turning green and the blast of the horn from the car behind you. Then there's the old joke about a doctor telling a patient he only has six months to live. When the poor man gets the doctor's bill, he tells him he can't pay it. So, the doctor gives him six more months to live! Here are some more quotes, which, if you try to analyze them, sound kind of weird (are they even true?):

'The time has gotten away from me"

'Take time to smell the roses along the way'

'Time is of the essence'

'Time waits for no man'

"I don't have time for that today'

'Time heals all wounds'

'It's high time you did that'

'He has way too much time on his hands'

'Take time to unwind or relax'

Here's a somewhat related topic. As I continue to age, I find myself constantly getting side-tracked around the house (going into a room to get something and, having arrived, forgetting why you went there is a totally separate discussion – like forgetting why you walked into a short- term memory clinic!). I'll start a project, get side-tracked, and hours later realize I have never finished the first one. Where has the time gone? Everything seems to come full circle in our lives, doesn't it? Is getting side-tracked such a waste of time? I don't think so because as long as you're accomplishing other tasks in between, within that timeframe, you're doing fine. I mean, these other things needed doing also, right? After all, only God can really decide when your 'time' is up!

Speaking of the word 'up', I can't believe how many different uses and meanings it has. Why do we wake Up each morning? Why do we call UP our friends, or warm UP the leftover food, or write UP a report for work, or brighten UP a room, or clean UP the basement, or lock UP the house before we leave, or speak UP when called upon? How can someone stir UP trouble, line UP for tickets, work UP an appetite, or think UP an excuse? Best of all, who used UP the toilet paper? Today's kids often greet each other by saying, "What SUP". I think by now, I'm pretty mixed UP!

Why do many senior citizens have absolutely no peripheral vision at all! If you're not careful, they'll walk right into you - sideways! Is it a function of arthritis and they can't turn their neck to look around, or is it a visual thing? Some people seem to be born with the malady, while with others it's definitely acquired behavior. In any case, a lot of fender benders could be avoided if they made an effort to look around first. This brings up the topic of contending with older drivers on the road. I thought I saw one of those new 'self-driving' cars the other day when, in fact, the driver was a little old man too short to see over the steering wheel. When is it time for people to stop putting themselves and others in danger by getting off the road? Obviously, it's an individual thing wrapped up in the second amendment to our constitution. If you haven't maimed or killed anyone recently with your car, you have the right to renew your license and continue to drive. Ah, there's the answer! We only require road tests for new, first time drivers – maybe we should insist on road tests for everyone over 70 (or whatever age is agreed upon). At least require them for drivers under four feet tall!

Is it just me or do other older men have recurring night dreams about desperately trying to find a bathroom? It usually involves roaming through a mall or strange building trying to hunt down a urinal. The only other truly 'recurring' dream I recall ever having involved not being able to locate the room where my final exam in college was taking place – probably because I had skipped the class so often, I forgot where it was. Undoubtedly, the 'bathroom' dream is caused by an aging prostate and the medication I am are taking to alleviate this condition. Perhaps this would explain why my wife has never mentioned having a 'bathroom' dream'. I think she is aware, however, when I'm having this dream because before I have an accident, she'll wake me up and point to the bathroom while politely saying, "It's that way, honey, don't you remember - you were just in there 30 minutes ago?" Some women might justifiably ask their husbands, "How come you have to get up three or four times each night to use the bathroom?" A sarcastic response might be, "I dunno, I guess I must enjoy being sleep deprived all the time!" At the risk of self-embarrassment, I have admitted to my close male friends (and now the world) that I have begun to carry a plastic urinal in the trunk of my car for emergencies while on the road. It's the same deal as having flares, blankets, water bottles, a reliable car jack, etc. I'm glad I have that 'bladder back-up kit' handy. One time on the drive back from Florida, I found myself stuck in a long traffic jam on I-75 with no exit in sight. The line of cars and trucks stretched for miles. It's very difficult and uncomfortable to drive with your legs crossed for hours. Suffice it to say, that urinal was a life saver! Betty Davis is quoted as saying "Getting old isn't for sissies". My mother used to say, 'It's no fun getting old, that's for sure". What a classic understatement that was!

Why do you see a lot of really old people (especially in Sunset, Arizona) walking (some actually shuffling) around in a grocery store with their mouths permanently hanging open? Are they actually sleep-walking, or in a coma, or do they have an adenoid problem? Some of them look like actors from the TV series 'The Walking Dead'. Have they recently 'busted out' of the nearby neighborhood retirement home (some of them look like they're wearing pajamas, which is perhaps a far cry better than a night shirt or nothing at all)?   Maybe the open mouth has to do with their false teeth not fitting properly or mistakenly wearing someone else's fake choppers (after all, the Tooth Fairy now owns more of their teeth than they do).   I definitely think those motorized carts that people wiz around the grocery store in should have turn signals and 'beeping devices' to warn the other shoppers of their approach.   At the very least, they should carry a license to drive them.   Can you purchase specific insurance to protect yourself from being mowed down or pinned between the fruit and vegetable sections of the market?   You or a loved one could easily be maimed for life!   I'm currently checking the courthouse records for pending litigation involving 'hit and run' or electric cart speeding infractions within stores.

Why do lots of old people who are hard of hearing (pretty much deaf) talk so loudly?   Do they think you can't hear well just because they can't?   Does squinting your eyes and dropping your mouth open while moving closer to the person talking really improve hearing and understanding what the other person is saying?   Granted, it is difficult to take part in a conversation at a restaurant with a lot of loud background noise.   It's also difficult to hear when you're outside and an airplane roars overhead or jack hammers are breaking up a street in front of you, but for Heaven's sake, if you're having trouble, please give us all a break and get a pair of hearing aids.   They're covered by Medicare!

There have been television commercials running for some time centering on the topic of male impotence. One in particular is really strange. It depicts a man and a woman (I think, because you only see their backs) each sitting in their own bathtub outside in the yard.   They are facing away from the camera, staring at the sunset overlooking a lake or perhaps the ocean. I think they might be holding hands as well. I don't get it. What does it mean? Are they in their own front yard or on someone else's lawn?   Does taking the manufacturers pill give you the urge to expose yourself by taking a bath outdoors? If so, how are the water lines connected to the tubs? Is yearning for the fresh outdoors merely one reaction or side effect? Is there any fine print or a disclaimer at the bottom of the screen to warn you? Do they put a side effect warning label on the prescription bottle itself?   What other behavior could result from ingesting this product? Might you commit some inappropriate act that would get you sued or put you directly in jail? It doesn't appear there's even any water in the tub. What the heck are they supposed to be doing? The possibilities boggle the mind.

I've noticed while in Florida that many of the older people (winter visitors) will often remark, "I'm not sure what day it is". Now, for the most part, you and I know many of them are being facetious. What they mean is, one day is the same as the last or the next, so the days sort of blend together. Same activities, same routines, meals, etc. That can happen to retirees. Some of them, however, are serious – they really and truly can't remember the specific day or what they just had to eat or who they just spoke with. I think that's why they repeat themselves, as I apparently do, and tell the same boring stories over and over. Are they to be pitied or admired for being honest?

And while we're on the topic of Florida condo developments, I once found myself standing outside the locked clubhouse glass door while a monthly board meeting was just getting started. I was standing there with my legs crossed, desperately needing to use the bathroom. No way were they going to open that door. Somehow, they knew I was one of 'those renters'. Did they expect me to go in the bushes or, worse yet, in the pool? C'mon, at least the older men staring at me should understand prostate issues, after all. The enforcement of the by-laws and rules can sometimes go too far. One time, I dropped the pool access card and it fell through the wooden slats in the walkway near the gate. I couldn't get it out and was told I had to pay another $10 for a replacement card. Seriously? Outrageous, I thought! Instead, I planned to sneak out late at night when everyone was fast asleep and pry up the boards to retrieve my card. My wife looked at me sideways and I discarded that plan. Some communities really don't want the renter's grandkids staying over-night when they come to visit. What are the poor kids supposed to do, sleep in their car or in a lounge chair by the pool? The 'no saving chairs' deal at the pool often creates some tense, but humorous scenarios as well. One day, two guys reached for the same lounge chair and in the ensuing struggle, nearly threw out their backs. Then you have the posted 'Pool Rules'. Rule #1 states, 'please shower before entering pool'. I don't think it's an issue of hygiene as much as having your sunscreen lotion wash off in the pool. So, the alternative is you're going to exit the pool with a bad sun burn, right? The lobster skinned seniors are probably the bathers who actually obeyed these rules. Another rule actually says, 'Do not swallow the pool water' – really! It's a salt water pool with different chemicals. Strange bacteria could be thriving and lurking in this environment, in addition to the sun tan lotion 'oil slick' floating on the surface. If you drank the pool water, you'd probably throw-up right into the pool which would cause others to toss their cookies resulting in a contagious mass epidemic. Either way, not drinking the pool water is probably a very good rule – besides, you can never be sure if a bather actually made it to the bathroom in time. If you're really thirsty, there's a drinking fountain nearby. Yet another posted rule says, 'No food or beverages in glass containers allowed in pool area'. Keep in mind, many of these older folks sitting around the pool deck are minus their glasses and hearing aids. They aren't as 'spry' as they used to be either. If they aren't paying attention, they could fall right into the pool and possibly drown! If they cut their foot on a broken piece of glass and then fell into the water, they could be attacked by a great white shark (remember it's a salt water pool)! Their friends and neighbors may not even hear their distress cries for help! Later that evening after dinner, "Where's Harry?" - "I dunno, the last time I remember seeing him he was treading water in the deep end as a dorsal fin circled him." Another standard pool rule is 'No diving into the shallow water'. Shouldn't some degree of common sense prevail here? The same goes for 'Do not use the pool during an electrical storm or tornado'. In Florida they have a classic saying – "When you hear ambulance sirens wailing, it means another condo is about to go on the market for sale!" Sadly, I get it!

Perceptions and expectations are interesting as well. I've heard 'snowbirds' in Florida complain about 65-degree weather in February when, back home in Frostbite Falls, Minnesota (may not be a real place), it's minus 20 degrees, they have a foot of snow on the ground, and the icicles hanging from the roof gutters could impale anyone coming to the front door! When it gets down to 45 degrees, they close the schools south of the Mason-Dixon line. When the pool temperature is less than 86 degrees, they're freezing and complaining! Someone should remind them that 86 is pretty warm (and is also the median age of the residents in their community). When the pool attendant posts '86' on the chalk board, I'm not sure which one he's referring to!

Many times, I guess we don't realize how thankful we should be. I'm so grateful to have the chance to get away from the cold weather in the north and spend some time in sunny Florida that I feel guilty, and I'm almost jealous of me!

Based on extensive personal research and experience, I've come to the conclusion that there are three categories of old people vacationing in Florida during the winter: 1) Just recently retired and eager to enjoy hobbies, interests and travel, 2) Getting older, enjoying life, not venturing out as much but still cognizant, and, 3) Really ancient, feeble, and exhibiting borderline dementia. While I definitely consider myself firmly belonging in category 2, there are many who, sadly, have slipped into #3. For some reason, I seem to attract these people like a magnet. Perhaps I'm too kind or just a good listener. By way of example, there's the guy who excitedly proceeds to tell you the same joke over and over again, during the same conversation. He must have a tape running on a loop in his brain.

Don't bite the hand that feeds you ...

Apparently, many pet owners will go to great extremes in an effort to provide the very best care for their dogs. A case in point are the number of 'Pet Resorts' springing up around our area. Do you really need to send your dog to a 'resort'? Does this give you bragging rights in the neighborhood? One such grooming and boarding place (dare I use the word KENNEL?), advertises, "We're the perfect 'home away from home' for your dog when they need an overnight stay". Wait a minute, they don't really need all the luxurious treatment (pampering) they are going to get at this overnight stay, do they? They go on to say, "Dream Big and Stay Happy Always" – who's happiness are we considering here, yours or the dog's? Does a dog even know what true happiness is? Does the dog even care that he's going to get all spruced up? Do they encourage dating? "Going on vacation"? Treat your dog to one as well! – Your dog will spend the day enjoying supervised open play with their BFFFs (best furry friends forever), and their nights enjoying restful sleep – Unleash the Love!" Please - a bit extravagant and over the top if you ask me. For anyone who's visited a kennel, you know a restful night's sleep is a real stretch – what is this, The Waldorf Astoria? People who take their dogs to these 'Doggy Daycare' places must have money to burn. You know that if they stay there, they're bound to get 'kennel cough' and you'll be 'coughing up' even more money later at the vet. Another swanky, upscale kennel suggests the importance of an annual 'wellness exam' for your dog. Gimme a break! Do they want you to think that Medicare will cover this? They put out a newsletter which covers topics like: New Year's resolutions for your pet, summer safety ideas, National Dog Day, the right insurance for your dog, doggie ice cream treats on a hot day, geriatrics and pets with special needs, and, flee flea biscuits. I'm not making this stuff up. OK, look, I've owned dogs and loved them very much. They are very faithful, always happy to see you, never argue or disagree with you, offer great companionship, and can certainly seem a true part of the family – I get it. But, let's be honest here – they are not human beings after all, they are animals.

In my neighborhood, I'm more than certain I'm the oldest resident. This says a great deal all by itself! Most families are much younger and in the process of raising small kids. Almost without exception, each family owns a pet, usually a dog. Here's the deal I don't get. Very often, they have two dogs. When I tactfully ask the parents, "Why the need for two dogs? Isn't one enough?", their answer is that one dog gets lonely and needs companionship. Wait a minute, isn't that what people are for? Aren't they supposed to be each other's companions – man's best friend and all that stuff? You mean to tell me if the pet is left alone it will develop a psychosis and require therapy?

Legally, pets aren't dependents, so there's no tax exemption here. You could end up spending your entire paycheck feeding two dogs, especially large animals. On the other hand, one neurotic dog without canine insurance might cost you an 'arm and a leg'.

As mentioned earlier, dogs often provide great human companionship. This can be especially true for the elderly. Many area hospitals and assisted living facilities offer 'Pet Therapy' programs for those unable to own and care for their own pets. The hospital where I volunteer has a few therapy dogs (derived from the word therapeutic) who, along with their owners, routinely visit with many patients. Even patients suffering with dementia are delighted to spend time with a therapy dog or puppy in their rooms. A new twist on this program involves robotic dogs who can be affordably purchased to 'stand in' for the living pet. The cost starts at around $299. The latest model, the "Tombot" golden retriever dog, reportedly looks, feels, and acts like a real dog. It wags its tail when petted, barks when you speak his name, and moves its head, ears and paws. These robotic companion animals are designed to improve the quality of life for seniors and those with disabilities. Designed by the Jim Henson Creature Shop, it emulates a live animal's appearance and behavior. Children with allergies can now have a robotic dog in their home as well. You don't have to bathe them, take them for a walk at midnight, or visit the vet for costly shots. In addition, they never bite, there's no poop to clean-up, you save on the cost of a leash, no toys or treats to buy, and, you don't have to stock up on Alpo. The down side is you can't go for a run with him on the beach or hike in the woods – he's rather confined to the house. But, is he really happy to see you when you arrive home?   The more I think about this deal, there could be something very wrong with this picture!   As with all computers, they have a mind of their own. Wait a minute, what if they break down without any warning and turn on you? It's just you against the robot! Worse yet, what if he attacks you in the middle of the night – when you least expect it! Remember what havoc 'Gort' caused in 'The Day the Earth Stood Still'? Who's really in control here?   Who's the master and who's the companion? Some companion – you could be dead by morning! You might just find yourself in a new episode of 'The Twilight Zone' where he short circuits, goes berserk and kills the towns-people, and then comes back for you! You never know when he might go wacko or self-destruct, especially if someone accidentally got him wet. On second thought, I think I'll stick with old Fido or Spot until he dies of more natural causes!

Once, I was invited to attend a funeral for a friend's dog – ceremony, grave, headstone, the whole nine yards. To show sympathy and offer comfort, I asked how old he was. The friend said (holding back a flood of tears) 84. I didn't have the heart to ask if that was in dog or human years. For all I know, he may be listed in the Guinness World Book of records for being the oldest canine. I respectfully and politely declined the invitation – partly because I thought it was creepy (think Stephen King's 'Pet Sematary') and partly because there was no lunch being served afterward!

On a semi-rural road, several miles northeast of where we live, stands an old farm house surrounded by acres of land. It is still occupied and houses a business that has been in existence for years. The people who make this their home raise and sell alpacas. There is even a permanent lighted sign on their front lawn advertising these animals for sale. Now, I don't know about you, but I wonder how large a market there exists for alpacas and the individuals who would want to buy them? Apparently, they are not suitable as pets or around children due to the fact that they spit and bite! They are related to lamas and camels – hence the spitting issue. One is even in the Guinness World Book of Records for generating the longest cherry pit spitting distance! Just kidding. I'm told they live to the ripe old age of 20 years or so and prefer to live in groups or packs. Purchase one, and you could be stuck with them making quite a mess on your property for a long time! One web site lists 474 Alpaca farms in Michigan alone and these animals come fully guaranteed, whatever that means! The thing is, you're not likely to see them appear on a restaurant menu. Actually, it turns out they are bred for their naturally colored fleece and are shorn (is that a word?)

once each year to make yarn, blankets and rugs. I don't know what their favorite food is but each one costs between $500 and $1,500 to purchase. Shows what I know. By comparison, I wonder how much sheep cost today. Alpacas must be one of the most carefully guarded secrets in Michigan – who would have thought? This also explains why there is a 'No Hunting' sign clearly posted on the front lawn of the business. Really?

Many condo owners around the country own little dogs and they faithfully walk them each morning. They are cute (the dogs, that is) and, again, offer great companionship. There's an old joke concerning a woman who goes into an upscale pet boutique clothing store looking for a warm, cover-up type sweater outfit for her little dog. She can't find anything to suit her tastes (not the dog's) or the right size on any of the racks so she asks a sales lady for help. "Why don't you bring in the little darling for a fitting?" suggests the sales lady. The shopper explains, "Oh no, I couldn't do that, you see, it's a surprise!!" Probably not too far-fetched, right?

Have you heard woodpeckers at work in the evening trying to find insects in trees? Their heads are moving faster than a machine gun for hours on end. How can they have any brains left? Maybe they don't and that's why they occasionally mistake aluminum siding for a wooden tree trunk!

Is human nature really natural? ...

Why are many little children (and some adults) afraid of the dark? There's never really anything in a dark bedroom that isn't there during the daylight hours anyway, right? So why do some of us get nighttime 'heebie-jeebies" imagining 'things that go bump in the night'? It's probably just an over active imagination coupled with fear of the unknown. In my case, I'm sure it involved having watched way too many horror movies as a kid. The clinical term for fear of the dark is called Nyctophobia. The absence of light creates fear of what might be in, or concealed by, the darkness. When I was eight or nine years old, my youngest brother used to say, "I'm a-scared of the dark". I asked him why and he just repeated "'Cuz, I'm a-scared, that's why." Emotional anxiety can lead to irrational behavior. If you suffer from this malady as an adult, never tell another grown-up because they'll think you're looney and send you to a therapist and start you on meds! The truth has a basis in learned behavior and survival. We humans are not nocturnal creatures by nature. Cavemen learned the hard way not to hunt for food at night in the dark. Dangerous animals (who actually were nocturnal) also searched for food at night and you could be killed or worse! We learned to 'stay out of the dark' – 'there's danger there'. "Where's Clyde, he was just standing right here next to me". Losing your best friend in the dark will definitely scar you for life – or at least strongly encourage you to invent fire or at least the 'nightlight'!

So, what's the trick to not spilling an extremely full cup of coffee or tea while walking? You feel somewhat like a tight rope walker trying to balance high above the crowd without losing your balance and falling, don't you? After years of experimentation, I think I've discovered that the two are, in fact, very similar. Personally, for me, if I stare at the cup, I'm almost sure to spill it. On the other hand, if I look away while walking, it seems to stay rather level and doesn't spill - more often than not. Wouldn't you think the opposite? That is to say, if you focused and concentrated on the cup, wouldn't that avoid the spillage? Apparently not. I don't believe this phenomenon is age related either. Unless, that is, you are truly decrepit and have a serious case of the shakes. To complete this analogy, the 'high wire' performer looks straight ahead and not down at the ground. In similar fashion, if you look forward towards your destination, your chance of spilling the beverage is greatly reduced. I think this could be viewed as a small microcosm of getting on in life itself - to focus on where you're going (the important destination or goal) and not just surviving or getting through the moment. I totally get the message!

There was a television commercial that ran awhile back from Xfinity Corporation that was right on the mark. The gist of this spot involves the use of cell phones by an entire family sitting down to enjoy a Thanksgiving Day dinner together. Everyone (except Mom) is seated around the table, the food is ready to eat, and, you guessed it, Dad and all the kids are staring at their phones. Enter Mom who looks directly at the camera while pushing the kill switch on the wireless connection. She has succeeded in halting the use of all the phones simultaneously. Having gained complete silence (and the shocked attention of all), she glances around the table smiling and asks "So, what's new with everyone?" This is great (and long overdue) because it delivers a not too subtle message and reminder of why we gather together for a holiday meal in the first place! It also suggests that many people think nothing of acting rude around others, including their immediately family! Maybe this is typical behavior for them. Maybe they have never been told bluntly that they are being rude. The truth is, they are probably clueless. One of them could have died and the rest would be oblivious! If Mom hadn't taken the initiative and brought them all to their senses, we're led to believe there would have been no communication at that holiday meal whatsoever. This commercial is obviously humorous, but it points out an example of a change in values in our culture. Do you think it would have happened if Grandma or Grandpa had been at that table? Now, I don't want to start an argument here about parents not teaching their kids how to behave properly (after all, Dad is joining right in).   My point is (also something I don't get) why does it seem people are becoming so rude to each other?

Yet another commercial (offered by Aflac Insurance) contrasts the cost of plastic surgery for a family member with the cost of an upcoming planned family vacation.   Here's the premise.   Dad has seriously injured his face in an accident and is in obvious pain. Mom and her young son immediately question whether his face should receive medical attention or they should continue with their plans to visit Hawaii.   Apparently, the conundrum is they cannot afford both. Again, it's definitely creative and funny on the surface, however, do young kids watching really receive the appropriate message? Are these TV parents demonstrating or teaching them good behavior? Why doesn't anyone attend to Dad's bleeding face or offer some semblance of empathy or concern? No one has even offered to drive him to the clinic. The overriding feeling we are left with is a genuine lack of concern for what's really important at the moment and in life in general - how to show proper concern and comfort, make good choices, and then arrive at the proper decision. If I don't stop here, I'll really be branded an old fogey (if that hasn't taken place already).

While we're on the topic of rude or dangerous behavior, I feel I must share my pet peeve with you. Does it bother you to be driving along at the speed limit and have another car riding your bumper mile after mile? My wife will tell you that I complain about this practice daily. Why do these drivers create such dangerous situations? Why don't they just go around you (or better yet, slow down)? Do they have a death wish? Do they want to take you with them? Did they not get enough time playing 'chicken' as a kid while riding their bike or engage in 'bumper cars' at the local fair? It's even worse with large trucks. They're glued to my rear bumper and when I look in my rearview mirror, all I can see are the big letters 'MACK'. It's scary and I don't get it! There's absolutely no way they could stop in time if I had to slam on my brakes quickly (like if a little kid or animal ran in front of me). Why would they take a chance on being involved in a serious or fatal accident? Do they make a practice of living on the edge all the time? Do they even realize they would be totally at fault and held accountable if there was an accident? The other driving situation that really gets me is when a person is so impatient that he (or she) can't wait to zoom around you. My only satisfaction is when I coast to the next stop light a half mile up the road and they're stopped right ahead of me at the same light. What's the rush? Where do they learn this behavior?

Is it always important to be right? Can't we acquiesce to another point of view once in a while or at the very least, agree to disagree? I think it's much better to be kind, generous, and, forgiving than to be right. By the same token, why do some people have to be serious all the time? It is said there is a time and place for everything.   There is a time for levity, fun, and, general silliness as well.   I don't really understand why many corporate managers put so much pressure on themselves to succeed.   I learned years ago that the pathway to grow as a person, and achieve success, involved surrounding myself with people much smarter than I was.   Give them the correct direction, goals, motivation, and, incentives - then let them take the bit in their teeth and run with it.   In the end, don't try to take credit for your success, give credit to others for making you successful.

Why does a baseball manager have to make a special trip out to the mound to inform everyone (and more specifically the current pitcher) that he's decided to make a pitching change? Can't he just waive a white flag or simply text him from the dugout?   Everybody paying attention would know he's had enough, right? Does he need the exercise? Why all the drama? You always feel badly for the pitcher involved, so why make things worse by trudging out there and drawing all the attention to it? Is it a power struggle deal when the manager gets to say, "Give me the ball"?   Even the announcers on TV and in the ballpark have to blare it over the loud speakers.   Can't the pitcher quietly and discreetly crawl off the field?   Can he get special counseling to avoid feeling guilty or inadequate?   Is there a 'team shrink' waiting to talk to him in the dugout? What about the new guy coming in to take his place?   Does he empathize with the first pitcher? Does it bother him to know he might get the same embarrassing public treatment as his predecessor? How sad, and it happens over and over – day after day, year after year. At the very least, a better approach would speed up the game which takes way too long to play as it is already.

Why do we pay good money (or bad money, whatever that means) to be scared to death by going to a creepy horror movie? There are a lot of scary things that are absolutely free! You could dangle off the edge of a cliff. You could sneak up on your spouse and yell "BOO". You could decide to go play in freeway traffic. You could run with the bulls down a narrow alley in Barcelona, Spain. You could drive your car on a twisty asphalt road with hairpin turns while blindfolded. You could host a holiday party filled with family and friends – now that's really scary!!

For me, there are three great smells in life: Raw gasoline, freshly ground coffee beans, and, a bakery shop. My wife would probably agree with two of these three. Actually, walking into a Yankee Candle store ranks right up there as well. Research has shown that our sense of smell evokes more memories of our past that any of the other senses. I can still hear my Mom's voice or my Dad's whistle, I can still remember what it felt like to touch a really hot surface for the first time, and watching a sunset reminds me of the first one my wife and I shared when first married, but some smells instantly transport me back to an event in my childhood. You don't even have to try to remember, it just happens. Funny how that works, isn't it?

Why do large conch shells forever have the sound of the ocean inside them? At some point, doesn't that sound go away? It's pretty cool to demonstrate this phenomenon to your little grandchildren. Personally, I'm afraid when I put the shell up to my ear some snail-like creature will dart out and scare the daylights out of me! Or, worse yet, crawl into my ear and eat my brain! It is said that "nothing lasts forever', but apparently this is one exception.

George Carlin was a very funny comedian – wait, that's redundant, isn't it? His humor and jokes had a strong sense of truth to them, sort of like a modern-day Will Rogers. In any case, here are some of my favorite Carlin quotes:

"Religion is like a pair of shoes, find one that fits for you, but don't make me wear your shoes".

"In comic strips, the person on the left always speaks first".

"There's no present, only the immediate future and the recent past".

"The best definition of 'instantaneous' is the time between the light turning green and the car honking behind you".

"Weather forecast for tonight: Dark".

"If a dumb person gets dementia, how do you know"?

"What does it mean to pre-board? Do you get on before you get on"?

Carlin also said he could do without the following people: (1) A guy in his late fifties named 'Skip', and, (2) Couples whose kid's names all start with the same initial. Funny 'stuff'!

We recently took the grand-kids to the zoo.   They have a very nice pontoon boat ride around islands inhabited by different species of monkeys and lemurs.   When you reach the front of the line and are ready to board the boat, a zoo employee tells everyone to be respectful of those around you. Does this infer some people have been rude and obnoxious to fellow passengers?   It must be the case or they wouldn't caution everyone on the boat.   Did they witness people fighting or arguing? Did someone get pushed overboard and drown or get eaten alive by piranhas or alligators? Why can't everyone pipe down and let everyone enjoy the trip? I don't get it.

I've pretty much stopped watching most of the local news on television. It seems all you see are a lot of shootings, muggings, car jackings, robberies, murders and general mayhem. I'm not referring to all of the commercials, but the real-life stuff! A lot of this violence is captured on video by witnesses with cell phones (how do these people just happen to be in the right place at the right time?) or the police car camera. Almost daily, it seems, a driver is pulled over by police for committing some infraction of the law. Often, a heated argument ensues, resulting in a scuffle with the officer(s). During the altercation, punches are sometimes thrown and the driver gets cut, bruised, bloodied and generally 'beat up' while resisting arrest. Not the best (or most flattering) picture for a mug shot. Here's what I don't get. Without exception, when the prisoner is finally subdued, restrained, and placed in the back of the squad car, the police officer gently places his hand on the top of this guy's head to protect him from bumping his noggin. Why bother? The perp is already battered, bleeding, and half conscience and the cop is worried about him smacking his head? Would you want to be the next person to ride in that back seat? Does somebody clean it up before the next shift?

Hey, I know, let's have a garage sale ...

Neighborhood garage sales are a piece of enduring Americana as well. I don't know why I'm drawn to them, but they can be quite an interesting experience. As a potential buyer, you have to get there early, otherwise all the really 'good stuff' will be gone. If you want to attract men, you have to have power tools, electrical wire, old car parts, toothless saws, or old fishing tackle or tool boxes (actually just pieces of rusty metal will do!). Women shoppers are more discerning and professional. They will sort through dress patterns, cloth material, children's books or toys, and dusty old drapes for hours. Even though things are clearly marked for sale, people will point to something hanging on the garage wall (or attached to the roof) and ask, "Is that for sale?" Later on, as they're leaving, they'll point to the same object and say, "How about that?"

Shortly after we were married, my wife decided to hold our first garage sale. It took days (and many trips carrying stuff up from our basement) to prepare for the event. I 'poo-pooed' the whole idea, thinking it wasn't worth the effort and we wouldn't make a dime. Much to my surprise, hundreds of people showed up and actually wanted to buy our stuff! I smelled success so I immediately went into the house and started ripping everything I thought would sell off the living room walls. It was a frenzy! Two

147

women who couldn't speak much English showed up and asked if they might use our bathroom. My wife said "sure". A half hour later, I bumped into them in the kitchen and wondered if I should offer them coffee and something to eat as well! When they subsequently left the house (through the front door) one turned around and told my wife, "You live CLEAN". I couldn't help thinking, 'compared to what'? I also wondered if she was really an interior decorator in disguise from somewhere in Eastern Europe.

Generally, there is no trash or garbage collection on a holiday or weekend - the next pick-up is usually postponed to the following business day. My question is how do the workers ever catch up? I understand how overtime works, but how do they ever really make up that missing day? How much do they get paid for not working? Slice me off a piece of that deal!

When we originally built and landscaped our house, we planted a bunch of viburnum shrubs around our deck. The plan involved hiding things from view that we stored under the deck. It readily became apparent that these shrubs grew prolifically. If you listened carefully, you could actually hear them growing during the night. In no time at all, they were climbing above the deck and were clearly taking over. I began to feel I was in a remake of "Little Shop of Horrors". I even had nightmares of them turning on me, enveloping our entire house, and waking up one morning to see killer pods forming like in the old horror movie 'Invasion of the Body Snatchers'. Having personally trimmed them three times each year for 20 years, I can honestly say viburnum can't be killed by man nor beast nor insect (nor blow torch). I think they have more lives than a cat!

My wife and I recently decided to redecorate our home. Painting, carpeting, new furniture, and, a new mattress and set of box springs. We didn't realize it at the time of purchase, but the new box springs were 4" to 5" higher than our previous set. When they arrived and we reassembled the bed with the new mattress, it was so tall that I couldn't climb into bed! I nearly dislocated my back and limbs jumping from the floor to get under the covers. My wife, always the patient and practical person, suggested we try it that way for a while to see if we would adjust to it. Two months later, we still needed either a trampoline, ladder, or set of fake stairs to get into bed. I tried a variety of running leaps, but to no avail! I was also afraid of falling over the edge in the middle of the night and maiming myself for life. Finally, enough was enough and when it became abundantly clear the situation wasn't going to improve by itself, we called the furniture store to see what our exchange options were. I shouldn't have been surprised when the saleswoman told us that a new set of box springs would cost me $300 – even though the ones we just bought were less than two months old! Everything is now back to normal and I have stored the pole-vaulting equipment in the basement (next to the old box springs set). Maybe the grandkids can use them to make a cool fort. Every time I hear the word mattress, it reminds me of the line Peter Clemenza had in 'The Godfather' when, during the Olive Oil War, he warned everyone "Sonny's goin' to the mattresses" – without the box springs.

In some local, wealthy communities, people are so conscious of social advancement, they will pay lots of money to move from a five-digit address to a four, or from a four to a three. I don't believe there are single digit residential addresses, but if they do exist, some homeowners would set their sights on them as well. It's solely a matter of prestige and bragging rights within their community. I've seen moving vans load up all the furniture to move just one or two blocks simply because of the loftier address. Hard to believe that having a goal like that would be so important to some in the larger picture of life, isn't it?

I just wrote out a check to pay my real estate property taxes. The areas funded are always listed on the tax statement: School debt, Parks and Recreation, Operating Expense, etc.... In addition to these are Zoo Authority and Art Institute. I don't get it - we don't even have a zoo or an art institute in our little town! Who's fooling whom? Does anyone really read these tax bills? Obviously, somebody has been pulling the wool over the eyes of the property owners for a long time! Why, I could probably sneak in items like annual City Manager's Pub Crawl, Mayor's weekly Pizza Night, or Councils Valentine's Day trip to Vegas, and they would be none the wiser!   Wait, I know, how about earmarking this money for fixing our decrepit roads and bridges!

My wife, and perhaps all wives, writes down a list of things to do around the house.   She keeps it in a prominent location, visible at all times.   Maybe it's just me, but it gives me great pleasure to cross off items when they're finished.   It also gives me great frustration when my wife crosses them off herself after I've done them.   It's just not fair.   What's really not fair is when the items are finally all crossed off, and suddenly a new list miraculously appears.   It's never ending.   I'll bet even when you die, the new lists keep coming!

You gain weight, you lose hair - get over it! ...

When I was a little kid, I battled a weight problem (who am I kidding, I've constantly struggled to lose weight most of my life!). I also wore thick glasses, had an overbite, and big ears that stuck straight out. What a horrible combination of maladies to try to overcome! I began to believe I was related to Prince Charles or had actually been adopted from an orphanage somewhere in Beijing! Needless to say, I was teased a lot in school. It didn't help at all when my Mother told people I was 'big-boned' or had a 'large frame'. The truth was I overate and was a fat kid. I got braces to straighten my teeth and went without the glasses when I could, but being over-weight was a real embarrassment. Just going to a store to buy pants was humiliating! I figured I had company because there were stores that catered to fat kids. One such local store was called the 'Big and Tall Shop'. What a joke! Why couldn't they just be honest and call it 'The Fat Guy Shop' or 'The Store for Hefty Chubettes' or 'Big Boys Boom-Boom Britches' or 'Baby Huey's Duck Drawers' or 'Ollies Ole' Fashioned Overalls' or 'Sam's Stretchy Slacks' or 'Nick's Enormous Knickers' or 'Ted's Titanic Trousers' or 'Gerry's Gigantic Garments' or Ernie's Expandable Enterprise' or Dick's Dunlap Duds', you get the idea. Normal kids wouldn't be caught dead in there!! I wanted to crawl through the floor

153

when the salesman (who could have dropped a few pounds himself) brought over a pair of ugly jeans for me to try on and said, "Here, young man, let's try on these 'HUSKIES' shall we?" First of all, he wasn't about to squeeze into these farmer's duds, I was. Secondly, they had tool loops sewn around the waist and were clearly meant to be worn by carpenters, brick masons, or, in fact, farmers. The kids at school had a field day when they laid eyes on those 'classic dungarees'. Suffice it to say, I got my fair share of teasing or 'bullying'. Obviously, it wasn't like I was trying to make a fashion statement, or create a hip, new look – they were all that fit! I guess what I really don't get is why I couldn't lose the weight and keep it off. Wasn't the daily embarrassment severe enough? How about the effects on my health? If I couldn't summon the willpower to do it myself, I should have insisted that my folks tie me to a wooden fence-post for a few weeks or make me run behind the family car for a few miles each day. Then again, there were probably child cruelty laws against it – even back then.

The latest effort to help slenderize overweight women (or men, I suppose) is a new undergarment product called 'shapewear'. This is not to be confused with 'sleepwear', 'leisurewear', 'activewear", or 'Tupperware'. Earlier versions included control top panty hose, maternity clothes with a stretchy elastic waist panel (of which I was personally very jealous), and the much ballyhooed 'Spanx'. You basically just reshape or reposition your fat! I've just seen the advertising video – it's not pretty nor for the faint of heart. You almost have to be a contortionist to get into this contraption. As I see it, the trick is how to quickly get out of it in an emergency. Like what if you have to use the bathroom. I can just hear the comments from the other women waiting an eternity in a long line to use the restroom – "She's been in there a LONG TIME, hasn't she?" "Yes, but she's probably trying to wrestle out of her 'shapewear'!" On the bright side, you can eat as much as you can force down while appearing to remain svelte! No more counting calories, going to the gym, or attending boring Weight Watchers meetings either. You can proudly go to the 'junior' or 'petite' size racks at Nordstrom's rather than be seen shopping at Dress Barn Woman or Lane Bryant. Are there any health issues involved with wearing this stuff? Does it push the fat up to your neck or face causing your eyes to bulge out (think rubber squeeze toy from the 50's)? How do you breathe? Almost sounds like a super girdle. Do you run the risk of being asphyxiated or exploding on the spot if you exceed the recommended wear time? What happens if the material is flawed or defective? You might become severely embarrassed by a sudden mushroom appearing on your backside! This reminds me of the old Saturday Night Live sketch depicting the Widette family who all had 'bulge-bottoms' and thought they were normal!

155

Why do men's pants, belts and waistlines creep higher and higher as we get older? The sight of an old geezer with his belt tightly cinched up around his chest sure doesn't create the right fashion statement, does it? It must have something to do with having a pot belly. There's no escaping the pain, agony, and embarrassment of trying to maintain a normal waist circumference under these circumstances. The opposite configuration must be equally painful. I'm referring to the stomach actually bulging or hanging over the belt. This is what happens when an old fogey attempts to maintain a normal location for his waist! He finds himself an honorary member of what I call 'The Dunlap Club' – meaning his belly done lap over his belt! The strain on the belt material must be enormous. If it ever 'gave way', well, let's just say you don't want to be standing in front of him if or when that happens! A button shield would offer some protection. Either way (high boy or low boy), this condition ultimately results in a 'bad back' accompanied by a series of never-ending visits to the chiropractor. Probably not covered by insurance or Medicare because it's a 'pre-existing' condition.

Why do some people take their bathroom scale with them on vacation? Pretty obsessive if you ask me. Isn't part of being on vacation enjoying yourself? Doesn't that include going out to eat? Doesn't the specter of having to 'face the scale' the next morning ruin the pleasure of indulging in some favorite food?

156

After all, you're on 'holiday', right? Isn't there time to get back on track after you've returned home? On the other hand, maybe losing weight is so difficult for many people they don't relish the thought of gaining back what's taken them a great deal of time and effort to lose in the first place. They can't stand the idea of going through it all over again. To my way of thinking, this paradox is part of some self-imposed guilt trip. I totally get it; however, shouldn't life be simpler somehow? Isn't life too short to beat yourself up over a piece of cheesecake?

I read where the Weight Watchers organization has started sponsoring vacation cruises. I think the idea is probably to help people avoid over eating while aboard the ship. Maybe I'm wrong, but don't a lot of people take cruises partly to enjoy eating the plentiful gourmet food offered aboard ship? Would they feel they were not getting their money's worth if they couldn't eat rich, fattening food three or four times a day while on the trip? Come on now, who would sign up for an expensive European cruise if you had to starve yourself, weigh in every morning, or count points all day? That's not my idea of a fun, memory filled vacation. Frankly, I think more Americans would ante up their money faster by having an 'all you can eat' style buffet on board! Not likely to happen, though, because these tourists would never leave the ship to see anything! They would be chained to the 'pig trough' the entire trip! The only pictures they would get would depict their fellow passengers reaching for the Tums.

"How was your river cruise through Germany?" - "I don't know, I was too bloated to get off the ship and go see anything."

Let's talk about the 'human hair experience', shall we? Why, as men get older, does the hair in their nose (and ears) seem to grow faster (and thicker) than on their head? Many of us older guys could probably use more hair sprouting on top of our scalp than elsewhere on our heads. On the bright side, if you are already bald, you don't have to worry about having a 'bad hair day'. You don't have to buy hair gel and other salon products. You've eliminated dandruff. Also, you can wear neat hats and caps and not have to re-comb your 'flat hair' when you remove them. Keeps your head warm as well. One thing I really don't understand, though, is why young to middle aged men decide to voluntarily shave their heads. Why are they rushing Mother Nature? Do they think they are more attractive sporting a shiny dome? Do they dislike combing their hair that much? Isn't some hair better than none at all? Are they trying to save money on haircuts? Won't they end up using more shaving crème and razors anyway? Does it take less time to get going in the morning? If they don't wear a topper, they're going to freeze to death in the Winter!

So, I'm in an elevator the other day, the kind that has two sets of push button panels, one on either side of the door. A lady gets in and says, "Would you mind pushing the 5th floor?". I smiled and gladly complied - then I thought, hey wait a minute, why didn't she just push it herself? I don't get it! Did she have a broken arm? Did she not know how it worked? Was she trying to start up a conversation? She probably didn't realize the buttons were staring her right in the face. While we're at it, I'm pretty sure they still rivet a 'maximum weight' sign to the wall inside the elevators. Should this be a cause for alarm? If the elevator you're on is packed with people, some of whom are very large, do you take the time to estimate combined 'gross raw tonnage' to make sure you are safe? If it appears to exceed the limit, should you go around the car and ask everyone to fess up? Never mind, there's probably a reasonable margin for error anyway, right?

I noticed a new yoga studio while driving errands in town the other day. It's called 'Intentional Yoga' and there's a large sign on the building. It made me wonder, "Is this as opposed to 'accidental yoga'"? Are you automatically required to strike a vriksasana pose or go into the navasana position as you get out of your car in the parking lot? Next thing you know there will be 'Intentional Yogurt' or 'Intentional Yogi'. When I looked it up, the company is also referred to as 'Intent on Yoga' which makes a lot more sense to me than 'Intentional Yoga'. Their web site says they offer lots of snacks for their members after workouts. Great incentive. Doesn't that sort of defeat the purpose of the exercise?

While driving past a strip mall the other day, I glanced over and noticed a pizza shop located right next to a weight watchers office. Isn't that sort of a self-defeating deal? How are you expected to stick to your diet while walking back to your car? Way too tempting. Doesn't anyone else see the dichotomy here? Maybe if you pinch your nose you won't be tempted. Here's something else that's strange to me. A local cardiologist is hosting a seminar advertised as 'How to get rid of your Belly Fat'. He is a board-certified heart doctor, claims to be a 'wellness expert' and plans to discuss "the latest scientific breakthroughs and methods that can help you permanently and safely remove unwanted belly fat while quickly reclaiming your health, your youth, and your life!" Wow, that appears to be a lot to reclaim – but sounds good so far. Who wants to keep their personal body fat anyway, right? Here's the weird part – it's being held as a free dinner seminar. He further advertises, "kick off the holiday season by learning how to TRULY take care of your body". Seriously? If these attendees already need to lose weight and shape up, why encourage them to show up and eat! Do we really have to offer them an incentive like providing them with free food to get them to do the right thing? In other words, if you don't feed me dinner, I'll just stay home and continue to 'pig out' until my cholesterol level reaches 600 and I drop dead. I'll remain over weight just out of spite, doc! Here's a death certificate you can pre-sign. Wait, here's a healthier incentive, why not hold the seminar at a fitness club and subsidize their membership?

Why do patrons of local fitness and health stores try to find a parking space near the store? Wouldn't you think they, of all people, would opt for the exercise by parking further away? I think it's one of those 'human nature' deals.

Apparently skipping eating breakfast could adversely affect the arteries of your heart and possibly lead to cardiac disease. Time Magazine recently printed the following information: 'A study of more than 4,000 people in the Journal of the American College of Cardiology found that those who had under 5% of their daily calories at breakfast were 2.5 times as likely as those who had large morning meals to have atherosclerosis, the hardening and narrowing of arteries, with early signs of plaque buildup.' Mom already knew that! Years ago, she was telling us how important it was to always eat a good breakfast. It was fuel for your body to start the day off on the right foot. She made sure we ate breakfast before we left the house for school. She sure was smart, wasn't she?

Toilets, both private and public, have come a long way. Most people probably thought they had died and gone to heaven when out-houses or 'privies' were brought inside the home. What LUXURY (and convenience)! The seat had to be much warmer also.   Some people, I'm sure, were understandably concerned about the prospects of the smell permeating their entire house!   What did they use as air fresheners back then – pine cones or kerosene scented branches?   What did they switch to from corn cobs and newspaper?   The guy who invented actual toilet paper on a roll must have really 'cleaned up'.   I thought we had really advanced with the concept of the self-flushing toilet.   Turns out ongoing advances are still being made. Now we have colored water and self-cleaning bowls.   The latest I heard about today is a lighted bowl, ostensibly, so we can see and find the toilet at night.   A plug-in bathroom night lite is no longer required, you can select your own bowl color from among a myriad of choices.   Maybe I missed something here, but were there a lot of situations involving people stumbling around, falling down trying to find the toilet?   Next, someone will invent the automatic self-wiping device! Again, what LUXURY!

It's a wonder everyone who uses a public restroom doesn't end up in the emergency room of the nearest hospital.   As clean and sanitary as it may appear, there are millions of germs lurking all over the place.   Even if you thoroughly wash and dry your hands after finishing your business, you're still susceptible to rampant disease.   This is beginning to sound like dialogue written by Woody Allen.   What I mean is, when you're finished, you have to touch the bathroom door to get out. Then you've re-contaminated your hands all over again!   You can use the wet paper toweling to grab the handle, but often it's a real stretch to reach the waste paper basket at the same time. Here's a thought, WHY DON'T THEY PUT HAND SANITIZER DISPENSERS OUTSIDE THE BATHROOM DOORS? All hospitals have wall mounted sanitizers throughout their facility – why not restaurants? Are they worried about the décor? After all, hospitals, clinics, and doctors' offices, quickly followed by restaurants, are the most likely places to pick up an illness, right? The thing I worry about is, despite the posted signs in the bathroom, how do you know the restaurant employees have actually washed their hands 'before returning to work'? I also wonder, why do gas stations lock their outdoor bathrooms? Are they afraid someone will actually clean them? Invariably, when I exit the bathroom at church, having just washed my hands, within ten seconds, someone wants to shake my hand. I don't want to appear rude, so I collect a new batch of germs by grasping his or her hand. "Hi, nice to see you again (hope I don't come down with diphtheria tomorrow)"! As a child, whenever we had lunch or dinner with my maternal grandparents, my grandfather would always ask us, "Did everyone wash their 'patties'?" He was alluding to the old nursery rhyme "Patty cake, Patty cake, baker's man, bake me a cake as fast as you can, roll it, pinch it and mark it with a 'B' and put it in the oven for baby and me." It worked!

Before we leave the topic of bathrooms, why are the vast majority of toilets manufactured with the handles on the left side (as you stand in front looking at them) – aren't most people right handed?   Is it assumed you are going to immediately reach for the handle to flush (with your right hand) while remaining seated?   Isn't it awkward to find the handle without seeing it? Don't you then run the risk of getting your bottom splashed? This might be popular in Paris, but, personally, I prefer to stand and then flush. Hence, the handle is on the wrong side!

Too much information ...

Remember when your only phone hung on the wall inside your house? Didn't have much room to 'roam', did we? They hadn't even thought up roaming charges yet anyway! The coiled-up phone cord only reached three to four feet from the huge, attached rotary dial unit. That's when a phone was, in fact, simply a phone. Not a camera, not an instrument to play games, not a social forum connection, not a weather locator, not a newspaper, not a time piece, not a map, not a photo book, not a calendar, not a calculator, not a phone book, not a message center, not a recorder, not a mail box, not a travel log or guide, not a record player or juke box, not a notebook, not a radio, not a book, just a phone to call and talk to real, living people! We even had party lines – phone lines shared with another customer of the local phone company. If someone was using the line, you had to wait your turn until the line became available. You often got a busy signal without the voice mail option. You could call the operator for information – a real person, yes 'Siri'.

Speaking of rapidly improving technology, why can't our local weather forecasters be more accurate? With 'Doppler radar' and storm tracking abilities, why do they get it right only half the time? Why does this 50/50 deal persist? Maybe they would try

165

harder if they only received 50% of their salary! Actually, there is a much easier and simpler process – just as accurate and less costly. If you live in Detroit, all you really have to do is see what's happening in, say, Chicago because that's the weather you'll be getting tomorrow!

As I've admitted and divulged earlier, I'm not the most tech savvy individual around. So, here's yet another thing I don't get. How does your iPhone know where you are - all the time? Sometimes I don't even know where I am!! My wife can simply look it up and tell me where I am. For me, it gives new meaning to 'lost and found'! Remarkably, you can find your phone if it's lost, (even if you're not) - instantly. I think it has something to do with satellites roaming the heavens. They have 'apps' for everything today. Reminder apps: take your pills, go to the bank or doctor, clean the house, get groceries, lock the house door, check the thermostat, close the garage door, etc.... Sure saves time writing down notes to yourself. Medical or Emergency alert apps: allergies, surgeries, I've just been in a car accident, I'm being robbed (auto dial 911), other traumatic situations (see: 'I've fallen and I can't get up' in an earlier paragraph). Soon, apps will be taking over and running your complete life for you. You can turn off your brain and it will do everything for you - if you've remembered to charge your phone that is. Future apps: take a shower or bath today (as if the smell wouldn't give you a head's up), go to the bathroom (if you haven't already had an accident),

166

go to sleep (with or without pajamas), wake up and get dressed (don't go outside naked), brush your teeth (or put in your dentures), etc.... This could evolve into something like, dare I say it, 'Big Brother is Watching'.

I've heard people refer to using a 'cloud' in connection with their cell phone and computer devices. Since I had no idea what they were talking about, I asked an expert (my wife) what this bit of technology was all about. I assumed it had something to do with the Rolling Stones song 'Get off of my Cloud'. Maybe a new offering from iTunes? No, wrong again. Apparently, they were talking about the iCloud which is a storage and computing service offered by Apple Inc. It provides a means to store data such as documents, photos, and music on remote servers for subsequent download to yet other devices. Way over my head. I'm told one of Apple's iCloud data centers is located in North Carolina. Why wouldn't they put it in London, England where it's cloudy practically all the time? On the other hand, what if it rains all over your stuff? What happened to safety deposit boxes at the local bank? What are these, 'remote servers'? Are they akin to butlers and valets who live off site? Almost everybody today stores phone numbers, addresses and other data on their phones. Not me, I still have a rolodex on my desk for business cards. Works great unless I'm not at home and need a phone number. No big deal, I'll just ask my wife to look it up on her phone. As far as today's technology is concerned, I wouldn't know anything about communicating if my very patient wife had not dragged me kicking and screaming into the 21st century.

The automotive industry has certainly made great strides involving vehicle safety. The technology they have created is truly amazing and is instrumental in saving the lives of drivers and passengers (think anti-lock brakes, air bags, collapsible steering columns, safety glass, etc.). The safety innovations introduced in motor racing have translated to much safer production vehicles. It's almost unbelievable to remember the unsafe conditions we experienced in cars as kids. In the late 1940's and early 1950's, there weren't any safety belts, padded dashboards, etc. If you were riding in the front passenger seat (who would let their kid do that today?) the only thing preventing certain death in an abrupt stop was the outstretched arm of your father or mother. Sedans had a little shelf behind the back seat, below the rear window. I used to lay across the shelf playing with my tiny army men and model cars. In an accident, I would have been a human projectile, flying through the cabin and then through the windshield. The creation of 'autonomous cars' is the next breakthrough. Uber, Amazon, and other big players are vying for the leadership role in these new vehicles. What I don't get at this point is the question of liability. Who's to blame in an accident? What a debacle for the insurance industry and a field day for the attorneys.

Some older people want to keep up with new technology while others couldn't care less (they probably have grandkids to turn to for help). All of our new cars have made tremendous advances in navigation, comfort, safety, etc.... By the time I sell or turn in the car I still haven't figured out half the new gadgets the vehicle offers (even though I've read and re-read the little glove box owner's manual).

As many times as someone has explained it to me, I still have trouble understanding how electromagnetic waves are captured and result in seeing a TV picture or listening to a radio program. How does something invisible, flying through the air at great speed, translate into a visible picture on a screen? Who was so smart that he (or she) figured this out? Was it like Sir Isaac Newton's experience with the falling apple deal (gravity)? It obviously involves the distance between the crests and troughs of certain wavelengths, but how did someone first make the connection and figure out its practical use? To me, it's sort of like religious faith – "...the substance of things hoped for and the evidence of things unseen". I have faith that I'll be able to watch the football game at 1pm on TV or listen to it on radio. If there is something wrong with the reception, I reckon I'll have to call the cable provider (if I can find my cell phone and remember how to use it).

Here's another thing I don't get. Why do traffic light signals have push button devises on poles instructing pedestrians to 'push to walk'? Who's kidding whom here? The traffic lights are all timed by computer programs, right? Is pushing a button really going to stop or interrupt the timing devise so you can safely cross the intersection? I've watched people press the button and begin to walk into traffic with the expectation of getting to the other side alive! Are they nuts? Our busy downtown area even has talking pedestrian signals now. These are a great safety idea – if you're blind or otherwise impaired. Shortly after they were installed, I found myself at a corner having a conversation with one until I looked around and there was nobody actually there.

The older I get, the more I'm confused by Daylight Saving Time. I remember reading it was first suggested by Benjamin Franklin almost 250 years ago and that it was meant to stretch out the days light during the winter months when it got dark earlier. If you think about it too much you can start to get confused. Do I set my clocks back an hour in the spring or fall? Conversely, when do I move them to where they originally were, or is it ahead? Does anyone really know what time it actually is anyway? It's all probably just an elaborate hoax or educated guess unless you are a Druid and live near Stonehenge! Without the innovative phrase, 'spring ahead and fall back', I would be completely lost and late (or is it early) for everything. I can't imagine what it must have been like to live in 1751 when we finally decided to change from the Julian calendar to the Gregorian calendar. Did New Year's Day really used to fall on March 25? It's all very confusing.

We have it pretty easy today compared to when I was growing up 'back in the day' (sounds just like some old fogey, doesn't it?). Today's society craves convenience, speed, and efficiency – instant everything. I think it all started in the 50's with Ray Kroc, McDonalds, and 'fast food'. Fitbits are great gadgets for measuring calories burned, steps taken, etc.... Google and Wikipedia are available to quickly look up anything you want to know (or remember). We used to marvel at an individual's ability to recall all kinds of trivial information at the drop of a hat. People prided themselves on having a sharp memory. Now you just look it up 'on line'. I'll get asked a question and before I can even answer, my wife has found it on her phone. And today you can do everything with your phone – well, almost everything. What I don't get is who has the time to input all this information you're looking up and is it reliable? Facebook and other examples of social media are probably suitable for keeping in touch and sharing new happenings with friends. I guess what I object to are people who post drivel like "I have a hangnail today"! Do they honestly expect people to sympathize with them? Give me a break! Kids should be especially careful what they post. They have no idea that it will be out there forever. Better they should put down their phones for a while each day and read a book or go outside to play with friends.

We have a new system at our Secretary of State offices. They are trying to use technology to speed up the driver's license and license plate renewal process. You can go on their website and reserve a spot or make an appointment. In theory this is a step forward. In practice it really doesn't seem to save time. I say this because when I arrived, I had to wait in a different line anyway! I suppose it actually could have been worse because they had no clear directions as to which line, of several, you belonged in. You could have waited in more than one line which would defeat the whole purpose. It's probably best to expect to devote at least a half a day in their office.

I received the first billing statement from a new credit card account we recently opened. For convenience sake, I prefer to pay my bills online, using my own bank's bill payment service. I called the company to verify the correct address to pay online because I knew it was different from the mail-in address shown on the statement. After a series of phone prompts, I finally reached a living, breathing person. I told him that I only had a quick, easy question. He kept me on the phone for ten minutes verifying who I was – what was my address, phone number, mother's maiden name, date of birth, account number, the names of all my children (in chronological order), what I had eaten for lunch, what make of car I drove, what movie I had last seen, the name of my favorite childhood pet, my favorite historical figure, my favorite flavor of ice cream, etc. I lost it and explained that I wasn't asking for a date or planning to hack my own account, I merely wanted the correct on-line billing address – an easy, generic, simple question. Finally, I told him if he wanted to get paid, he would have to cough up the stupid address! Then he started to actually get surly with me, reading their entire lengthy company policy, ad nauseam. I don't get it – wouldn't you think they would make it a lot quicker and easier to give them money?

Enough, already...

W ell, it appears we have mercifully come to the end of this little book (and not a moment too soon, either). I guess it's time I wrote something more serious.

It occurs to me that in virtually all religious faith-based organizations, the popular expectation and belief among members is that 'good people' go to Heaven – that good behavior is rewarded in the end. In the Old Testament, if you followed the laws of Moses, the 10 commandments, and obeyed what the Pharisees taught (that is to say, "If you were a good person"), you surely would end up in Heaven, right? Millions of people base their eternity on this premise. On the surface this might seem logical. In reality, these were only rules to live by, not a pathway to Heaven. A few years ago, author Andy Stanley wrote a short book called 'How Good is Good Enough?' In his book, Stanley discusses the problems with the philosophy or view that good individuals go to Heaven. Remember Professor Marvel using the expression 'good deed doers' in the movie The Wizard of Oz? One issue involves the definition of 'good' itself which you won't find in the Bible at all. There is no definition or yardstick to measure goodness by. You'll go to your grave wondering if you've been 'good enough'. Another is that this viewpoint is contradictory to the teachings of Jesus. If God were 'fair' he would give us what we deserve, that is, we, as sinners, would not be able to enter into the kingdom of Heaven. Fairness does not determine the truth. In other words, there are no 'good people', there are only sinners. Tough, sobering conclusion, eh? Oscar Wilde, the English poet/playwright, wrote, "The only difference between a saint and a sinner is that all saints have a past and all sinners have a future." So how do you get into Heaven? The answer is only by the grace of God through his mercy and forgiveness. With regard to consistency and fairness, everyone can meet the same requirement and get there the same way. In John 3:16 of the New Testament in the Bible, it states (to paraphrase) that God sent his son to be sacrificed for our sins and that if we believe in Him and his teachings, we will not perish but have eternal life. If we are willing to believe in Him, we have met the requirement. "That you believe Jesus is who he claimed to be and that you are no longer trusting in what you have done, or will do, will get you into Heaven". It took me a lifetime to understand this truth. I didn't 'get it', but now I do! The good news is that good people don't automatically go to Heaven − forgiven people do. If you have placed your faith in Jesus Christ as your savior, try faithfully to obey his commandments, live a life that is pleasing to him, and pray for his mercy, you are likely one of those forgiven people.

Acknowledgements

Many writers gratefully thank their wives, children, grand-children, estranged former relatives, co-workers, friends, acquaintances, and often, complete strangers for their support, advice, consent, and general help. For a refreshing change, let's be honest here. I had none of that! Apparently, everyone I showed this book to along the way had no sense of humor whatsoever. Not one person even cracked a smile. In truth, I wouldn't want to demean or incriminate them for participating. Anyone who has spent time in close proximity to me is familiar with my quick wit and unique sense of being funny, frivolous, silly and just plain goofy. Many people figure that to have a sense of humor means you're not a serious person. I maintain that life is too short to remain serious all the time (actually, at this stage of the game, I can now be serious for only about two minutes at a time). As stated at the beginning of the book, I generally see the humor in most situations. "It's a blessing and a curse at the same time..." said Barry Fitzgerald, the Irish character actor in one of his countless movies. In his book, "Shooting from the Lip", former US Senator Alan Simpson says his mother taught him that "humor is the universal solvent against the abrasive elements of life". Very true – but not used through ridicule, being hurtful, or at the expense of others well-being. I hope it will be said that I kept my unique sense of humor to the end. As Paul Simon wrote, "Still crazy (and hopefully funny) after all these years". In terms of real acknowledgments, I would actually like to thank my computer for not crashing, my memory for not fading, and my boredom for encouraging me to attempt and finish this project. Seriously, I do wish to thank God for every blessing I've been given and every opportunity I've enjoyed. I also want to gratefully thank my wonderful wife for her infinite patience with me over a span of nearly 50 years, as well as taking the time to review, proof-read, and edit this book. And a special thank you to my beautiful daughter, Kim, for laughing at my jokes and organizing my ramblings into a "proper" book.

As I get older, I'm reminded of many quotes and ancient sayings - none of which can be printed here. Captain Geoffrey Spaulding, better known as Groucho Marx, in 'Animal Crackers' put it best - "Hello, I must be going, I cannot stay, I came to say, I must be going. I'm glad I came, but just the same, I must be going. I'll stay a week or two, I'll see the summer through, but I am telling you, I must be going...".

All my best to you, except for any requested refunds on the purchase of this hilarious little book!

About the Author

Larry Perkins is retired and lives with his wife, Kathie, in Rochester, Michigan. He has two wonderful children and four precious grandchildren. He enjoys volunteering in the local community and at church. His interests include: Classic cars, genealogy, gardening, wildlife habitat preservation, reading, traveling, singing, and, best of all, spending time with his kids and grandkids, and laughing with his pals.

Made in the USA
Monee, IL
01 January 2020

19722064R00108